# Lost Treasure

by Pauline Edmunds

# Lost Treasure

by Pauline Edmunds



Edited by M.J. Silva
Cover by M.J. Silva



To contact Pauline Edmunds, please email:

diddycoy@hotmail.com
www.paulineedmunds.com

# Lost Treasure

**by Pauline Edmunds**

To all of the Voluntary Animal rescue services working relentlessly in Spain and around the world.

To AMY, my best girl in the whole wide world

# ACKNOWLEDGEMENTS

I owe this book to my two wonderful godchildren, Ben and Amy.

Ben for his openness to fun and adventure, his intelligent contributions in helping to design the book cover and insights to the storyline. And Amy, for her inspiring passion and love of animals. Her abundant love of life. Her flibbertigibbet creative imaginative nature, endless enthusiasm and support in helping me write this beautiful true story.

I wish to thank Monica, my dearest friend, whose ears I chewed in all the long distance storytelling phone calls. Her belief in my ability never floundered.

I thank my friend Ann for her support and for facilitating the perfect writing environment and Leonard for his wealth of knowledge of the English vocabulary.

A huge thank you to my friend Stella for her unending support and whose sharp eye for early editing has been so valuable.

A huge thank you to my brilliant editor M.J. Silva for her patience, guidance as well as her professional and flexible approach to my work.

Finally, to my close friend Philomena who encouraged me to 'just write from your heart'.

Pauline Edmunds

# INTRODUCTION

Long, long ago in the land of S*tray*, it is said in dog history that humans took wild wolf-cubs into their homes and reared them with their own children, with the result that they became easier to handle, made great guard dogs and were accepted as part of the family.

And over tens of thousands of years they became many different kinds of dogs you see today. Some bigger, some smaller, some fatter, some thinner, some long eared, others short eared, some long haired and others short haired.

They have pawed their way across this planet, covering many miles a day in search of shelter, food and water.

Pauline Edmunds

# CONTENTS

# Lost Treasure

# CHAPTER 1

# BENDOG RIDES AGAIN

"Did you bring the flask"? I called out to Nan, who had disappeared into the back of the van with my bag.

"Oh, and the front door key has jammed again", I continued, gritting my teeth and feeling impatient, after realizing it was probably due to my hasty attempt to retrieve it too soon from the lock.

I persevered, wriggling it around from left to right. *Oh! we must get another lock as soon as possible*, I mumbled to myself *and I won't be asking Laurel and Hardy, that local father and son team, for a hand either! What a right old stink they made of this one!*

*Qweeeekkty*. It was out! At last.

"T' be sure I have", Nan shrieked at the top of her voice, sounding like an early morning corncrake.

" 'Dat's dat done. Lord knows it's a bad night at'all at'all. We'll be glad of a hot drink later", said Nan. She sounded out of breath as she reversed her whole self from the back of the van, one leg at a time.

"Typical Irish weather eh? Wet, cold *and* windy." I moaned, pulling my jacket collar up over my ears.

*Growing a set of gills would be more appropriate.*

"Up boy!" I motioned to old Bendog, making sweeping movements with my arms from my thighs to over my head, drawing my hands up towards the back of the door.

For the first time ever, Bendog didn't seem to want to jump into the back of the van. I noticed he was staring straight at me. I dropped down beside him and his head drooped into my hands.

*Oh my!* I wondered.

Bendog's ears seemed smaller and thinner amidst the thin straggly hair that covered them and he was definitely hard of hearing these days, unless I stood close to him and yelled:

"BENNNNNN!"

He would look up sharply with an ok-ok-you-don't-need-to-shout expression on his face.

As I gently combed each one of his ears with my cold fingers, I noticed his eyes too. Each covered over in pale cloudy rings. In humans they call those cataracts. They were set back into their bony sockets, almost blotting out the dark wolf-like stare of his once bright and lively youth.

I lifted up his face. His teenage snow white fur that lined his nose and mouth was now grey. And his jowls, the folds of which were so many, lay like rolled blankets in the palms of my hands, almost white from old age. They seemed to portray a sad expression.

I gave him a quick kiss on his forehead.

"It's ok, boy! Come on!"

As I tried to lift his rear end over the step and into the back, Bendog pushed his body weight against me. So I shoved harder.

"Ppppuuuuuussssshhh!" Bendog finally arrived at his destination, his worn cushion on a side seat!

I could hear Nan in the front, by the odd *ooooh* and *aghh* echoing out into the dark night from the front cab. She was rarely without a moan or two these days, when a physical task was occurring.

I assumed she was trying to twist herself into a more comfortable position against the stiff material of the seat, before she finally settled down.

# CHAPTER 2

# A VERY EERIE SILENCE

As I fussed about in the back re-arranging my bag and bits, I could feel Bendog's eyes watching me - or my shadow - through the cloudy hue. There was an unusual *sshhhhhhhhhh* silence surrounding myself and Bendog which I just can't explain. And that I'd never experienced before in his presence. His stare, which I could just make out from the cab light spilling into the back a little, remained fixed on me and his nose twitched slightly.

Despite the wind blowing, a gale outside and the *flick a flack fleck* of the persistent rain falling against the back window, it was eerie and still inside the van. It was a moment I knew I'd never forget.

I thought I knew most of Bendog's moods by now, but this was a new one and one that I read to be a *I'd rather stay at home. I'm too old for this game.*

I guess he must have meant the game of travelling. After all he had a point. He'd travelled from Ireland to England, through France down to Spain and back so many times in his fourteen and a half years! So that night, perhaps, his show of resistance was marking a new chapter in his retirement.

But I had to return to England again to look after a dear friend's aged mother whilst her son had a break and the dear lady wouldn't entertain anyone else looking after her.

Nan and Bendog always dropped me off at the airport. It was our tradition. But I had been concerned about his deteriorating health recently. His hooligan days were well and truly over. He was a veteran now, a category he'd been allotted into when he attended at local dog show. He'd even won a rosette. I was very proud that day!

But these days, he would wobble over to a corner and just stare at the wall. His strong lean legs, now so worn - and arthritic according to the vet - from hours springing frogs and retrieving almost anything that was thrown for him, had taken its toll, resulting in needing much more time to get up off the floor, to stretch and walk.

My friend Mary, whose dog reached the same immobility, found an old doll's pram and she would take her dog out in it. Brilliant for them, but somehow I couldn't see my boy wanting to ride in a pram. He was much too proud, I'm sure of it. But still, it was pitiful to see such deterioration, and it was his breathlessness on exertion that worried me enough to make a vet appointment.

I was determined he would get the best care I could give him until the end. He deserved it.

."He's also nearly blind," I said to charming Dr Wilson. "And deaf." I blurted out to the vet when I had taken him for a check-up a few days earlier. I'm not sure why I felt the need to tell him that, but I did.

"Ah yeah, that's quite normal. It's what I'd expect given his age", replied Dr Wilson.

"I'll prescribe Bendog a tablet every day for his painful arthritis. His heart needs a bit help too, so there's another to take daily", he explained.

Dr Wilson's lofty stature towered over me and Bendog.

"And I really don't think he's up to long distance traveling", he called out as we exited his room.

*So no more great treks for you my boy*! I repeated to myself. I had prepared myself that perhaps he really wasn't fit enough to travel to Spain for our family summer holiday that year.

I would probably not go either if that was the case. I needed to be here for him. And with that last comment from the vet, I felt satisfied to leave the clinic.

Without fail, I could feel Bendog's lead at full strain. His head stretching out ahead pulling his tired body like a carthorse straining to pull a heavy load. Low to the floor he couldn't wait to exit that door.

He hated going to the vet.

# CHAPTER 3

# NAN TELLS A SCARY TALE

I was enjoying looking after my boy now he was old and worn. Pampering him and throwing the odd bacon rasher and pieces of rump steak in his direction. He'd sniff around the whole floor like a hoover until finally arriving at the tasty morsel, much to the annoyance of Nan. Her face would scrunch up and she'd click her tongue onto the roof of her mouth expelling a *tut! tut!* that always brought a cheeky smile to my face.

At least I could go over to the mainland feeling less anxious about my dog's wellbeing. The vet had said so.

"All normal for his age", he'd said.

Finally happy that every door, gate and window was all locked up, I jumped into the van. Nan was already sitting comfortably in her seat.

Her eyes gazed upon the road ahead, unflinching. Unlike myself as a passenger. If it was me, I'd be fiddling around in the glove box and tidying-up the console area. Or worse still - and much to Nan's annoyance - turn on the radio and travel through the entire spectrum of available stations.

*Cllckkjhhpppxxx*..."this.is"...*cccxpppp!ftt*.. "Dio"... *sqqqeeek.~~~.pffsssst*... "Good.ev"..*sssffeee*.... on and on until I found a quiet sounding voice or tune. Needless to say it was far from a modern version of a car radio!

Nan, now a silver haired grandmother of eight and a proud senior citizen was once a fully blown Irish girl of fourteen when she left her beloved homeland in search of work across the Irish Sea.

Her life on the Emerald Isle was carefree, with plenty of time to wander aimlessly amongst the Mountains of Mourn or to run for the messages, pushing neighbours babies in prams for miles and miles. Sometimes she had no idea of the time and she would find herself in fields a long way from home, jumping the stinging nettles or stretching her stick-like legs across a small stream, hoping she wouldn't fall in and get her lovely white new knee socks wet, trying to return home before the darkness ascended.

"Ah now…", she'd say to her audience, a portion of her small offspring staying at the wee cottage during a school holiday. She'd be leaning forward in her armchair as if she wanted to share a secret. And in a quiet slightly *trem…mm..morey* voice, she'd speak out.

" 'Wit'out the moonlight, the sky… was as black as a crow, and not a sound cud I hear about me. It was pretty…Oh...uuuuggghh", she let out a deep shudder. Her eyes shrunk to a squinting position and she'd bring her index finger and place it on her puckered lips.

" 'Aye...it was scary allrite childre', crossin' o'er 'der small bridges, imagining footsteps comin' up behind me, especially when I knew I hadn't passed anyone!"

At which point one or more of the entranced grandkids would call out.

"What happened Nanny? Was *someone* behind you?" A squeaky voice called from out of her watchful crowd.

"I.. eh, I didn't wait to…..eh find ooot", Nan replied. And she retracted into her seat as if the story had ended. But with one eye closed and the other one half open, scouring the room and waiting for the tension she created to flag, she suddenly jumped up.

"I ran like billeo!", she cried, "as fast as me legs would go. Me 'art beating like a captured burd until I reached me own back door."

She drew her arms up with her shovel-like hands spread open, pretending to push the door. And then she re-enacted, slamming it closed, pushing her rotund backside with full force backwards, both hands crossed over upon her chest, making the holy sign *phuu!...phuu!.Jesus! Mary* and the *price o' turnips* she cried out into the room!

Her breathlessness was evident of a last minute dash to get home safely.

*OOOHHH!*, cried the children in unison and *BWAHAHA!* as they burst into fits of giggles at seeing their Nan acting.

Yes, this was her childhood. She feared only the Priest. Other than that, she was a healthy cheery girl. Helpful, loving and giving with a bit'o a wild imagination.

# CHAPTER 4

# DOG SENSE

As Nan and I turned from our drive onto the country road heading to the airport, the empty trees that filtered the winter sun towered like enormous blurry statues over our little camper. The swirling curves of the hidden road ahead sheltered the thick bare briars and sally bushes. Their nude buds undisturbed, waiting for the first sign that spring had sprung and all of nature to gather at that precious moment and burst with new life.

Although it was just an airport run this time, sitting in the front seat always made me smile, even at this time of night. And before the engine had had enough time to warm up, we started our usual rendition:

*On the road again*
*Just can't wait to get on the road again*
*Goin places I've never been before...*
*dooo doo do.do do.*

Nan joined in her usual out of tune mode that always amused me. We sang along together until we both ran out of the words.

It was our ritual. It never got better. And it never got any worse.

But my joy only lasted for as long as the song.

My mind like a pair of pulled out trouser braces snapped me back to the image of Bendog and his strange behaviour earlier.

"I don't know what's wrong with Ben." I remarked to Nan. "He didn't want to get in the van".

"B'jesus and the price o' potatoes! Dat's a furst!" she replied.

"I'm not sure if it's because it's three o'clock in the morning and the light's bad here, but when I held his sweet face in my hands to… you know… to try and encourage him to get in the van, he didn't attempt to pull away. He just stared at me. An unfamiliar stare! He looked so…so...well… OLD! His eyes narrowed, softened even, as if he hadn't a slight bit of energy left…" I paused. "Now I come to think of it he didn't even raise his head for a piece of buttered toast before we left!"

I covered the brake with my foot and then gently pressed it until we had slowed almost to a stop. Turning my head to Nan, our eyes met.

"I know you probably think I'm mad but… I got a feeling like… hum…like…emmm… like…he was ready to be left alone … you know?"

Nan's lips pursed and her cheeks lifted as she sucked them inwards as if expecting to tell a gruesome fact.

"Some dogs do go off on their own… you know… to die, don't they?" She explained quietly, the words barely left her mouth when I could feel the tears well up in my eyes.

Everything was suddenly blurry in front of me and my chest felt heavy inside, drowning in sadness. I had so often feared about, maybe, having to let go. It had been almost fifteen years since I opened that velvet bag and his little puppy head had popped out!

"It's gone so fast and a long time to love something so much", spoke Nan.

Leaving one hand steering the van, I wiped the salty tears from my cheeks with the other.

Nan took hold of my free hand, nodded to me and quickly turned her head towards the side window and stared into the bleak night. She made no sound, but from the corner of my eye I could see her chest rise and fall and her shoulders shaking up and down like she was trying so hard to stay strong and stifle her sorrow.

"Go, you." She quickly grabbed at her handkerchief and pushed her nose into it. *BBBBLLLUUEEEEEFFFFMME*, she blew. With her nose clear, she continued.

"On ahead Jack, we've a long way t' go yet!", encouraged Nan.

My foot hit the gas and we were on our way again.

Although we didn't have Bendog neutered until he was older, I was now regretting that decision and bemoaning the reality that we would not have his offspring to continue his line.

We would probably be looking after his grandchildren by now. My head was full of *what ifs.* True sentimentality at its best!

"I know," said Nan in her soft Irish voice "we'll never know if der arr any little Bendogs running around here or in Spain!"

"He's certainly been around!" , I replied.

"I know it's hard for you. It's hard for all of us, Jack, but what *do* you want me te' do if some ting does happen... you know... while you're away in England?"

Deep down in my heart I dreaded that question and there it was. The reality was fast closing in on me. There was no way I could take Bendog to the vet unless he was suffering badly. Ideally, I'd rather he found a nice cosy spot around the cottage somewhere, lay down and went to sleep forever here in Ireland, where he spent most of his wonderful life. That way I could bury him near me.

"Do err..." *snif*, "emm... oh... em..."

My voice squeaked in a weak drawl as my sobs deepened.

"Emm....what errr ..."*snif* "...you have to do..." was all I could mumble amidst a mountain of tears streaming as fast as the rain outside ran down my face. As we turned the corner and headed off down the main drag, I sobbed.

”Just make sure….he.. he …errr… comes back to me.”

Nan paused for a while.

“Of course love, of course”, replied Nan lifting her hanky to the corner of her eye.

Suddenly a cold wind blew across my shoulders from behind.

# CHAPTER 5

# MISTAKEN IDENTITY

"Come on, quickly, get in, I'm going to be late for choir", I shouted to my two godchildren Matt and Lucy as they dawdled up the street bickering with each other over who should or who shouldn't carry the beach bag.

"It's not Manana, just because we're in Spain you two", said their mother Kathy, her hand flapping in the air and pointing to the side door which she'd opened in ready for their departure.

"Jack's in a hurry!"

*BANG! BANG!* A rather noisy grating sound.

*KREECCKK!!* The heavy and stiff sliding door of our campervan - which always needs a hefty heave *ho!* - locked into position, suggesting that everyone was now on board and all doors were firmly closed.

"Belt up, kids," I cried over my shoulder as my hands fumbled and bumbled their way to dismantling the tin foiled Coca Cola windscreen sun cover that had become stuck to the lopsided visor. *At least it keeps the steering wheel cool,* I justified to myself. Although then, in a panic to be on time for Roger's rehearsal, I would have steered a red hot poker!

"Air con coming your way, now!" I screeched over the *voorrr…voorrr* of the engine.

I stretched my hand to switch the desk top fan to *on*. It was a contraption that a previous owner had firmly fixed on the dash. Primitive yes, but effective, if only for the front passengers. At least I was hoping it would give a sense of cool air wafting into the back. After all, it was only 9 a.m. on this glorious August morning in Spain.

But with the sun lying in wait, it wouldn't be long before we would all be moaning and groaning, desperate to disembark from this overheating motor in dire search for a cooler shadier spot.

My foot was firmly placed on the accelerator. I pressed down hard.

*VOOORRRRRRR!*

I was just about to pull away from the curb when in the distance, probably about a hundred yards on the pavement, was a lone dog, making its way along the path towards the van!

*GGGRAAACKT!* Hand brake back in situ!

To be honest, at first sight, I thought it was a mirage. Narrowing my eyes, I could see the image of my beloved Bendog, back in Ireland.

But as it picked up speed and bounded with great enthusiasm, I realized it was a much younger dog. Although the same colourings and breed, it was definitely- and sadly - not him.

With the engine and time ticking over, I just couldn't take flight. By now, the dog had reached its target and the kids and their mother on the front double seat, bags and all, were all begging me to open the hatch, so they could greet the stray dog.

"Oh! It's a little Bendog" said an excited Lucy, her face beaming with delight. It was a name she had given him when she had just turned three.

"It's just like him, isn't it, mum?" I detected a quiet sadness in her voice, the hopefulness of a new discovery together with the disappointment that it wasn't Bendog.

Matt's inquisitive nature finally drew him from his seat and he perched his head on his sister's shoulder to make sure he had a good view too. Now there were four young smiling eyes peering down through the warming glass window to stare at this miniature, o*h Bendog.*

*Fwip..fwip..fwip...*The little dog's tail wagging, as it too stared up at the four smiling eyes.

"Well, that's impossible," asserted ten year old Matt, who unlike his sister's belief in magic, likes to stick to the facts.

"Spain is two thousand and six hundred miles from Ireland!", he announced.

"Look! It's wearing a collar", said their mum as she rolled the passenger window down to get a closer look.

Sure enough after a brief skirmish between the kids, who had suddenly developed superhuman strength, they managed to open the sliding door wide enough to disembark.

"PUUUULLLLLL!", cried Matt, when at most times he would grunt and groan at being expected to open from the inside.

Matt and Lucy quickly piled out onto the pavement, shoving each other from side to side as they surrounded this young bewildered - yet friendly - dog. It stood perfectly still.

It had its tail hidden under its belly, feeling intimidated, I imagine, from the hullaballoo caused by the excitement of the children's concern.

Its large amber eyes were focused on Lucy. As to who was qualified to identify this animal, Matt took instant charge. His long bony fingers scrambling frantically in and out of the dog's neck fur, until he was able to secure one finger under the collar, whilst he examined further for a name or any clue that would lead to its identity.

"It must belong to someone if it's wearing a collar, don't you think?" exclaimed Lucy who'd bent down onto her hunkers and was attempting to reassure the creature with a soft stroke of its head and fur.

The dog didn't move a muscle. It just stared at Lucy.

Its gentle amber eyes never left her face.

Pauline Edmunds

# CHAPTER 6

# LOVE AT FIRST SIGHT

"No, there's no name or any info on the collar", reported Matt.

I had remained at the wheel through all of this inspection and watched the antics of this episode from the side mirror.

*What a little treasure,* I thought.

The dog had a funny face, with straggly sticky- out ears and its amazing likeness to my darling Bendog.

In all of the dog behaviour books I've ever read, it states: *when approaching a stray dog. NEVER look the dog in the eye. Side up to the dog and wait for the dog to approach you. Put out the back of your hand for the dog to smell.*

That was nothing - of course - like we allowed our kids to do. They jumped out of the van as fast as possible, towered over the little animal and stared completely into its face, touching and feeling, being all over its nervous little body, half frightening it to death.

But all it did in return was a gently but insistently *slurp... slup...* over their hands, licking as if it had found a real tasty morsel of food upon their skin.

And its tail *fwip... fwip...* spinning in the air.

*So much for dog human behaviour!* I thought to myself.

However, as much as we all would have liked to have eloped with the dog into the back of the van, enjoying a spot of *criminal activity*, it suddenly dawned on me that we just couldn't take ownership of someone else's dog.

What if that was to happen to my beloved Bendog? What if he got kidnapped, just like we were thinking about doing at that moment?

No. It was wrong and I had to set an example. After all I had served Her Royal Highness as a Police officer years ago! *I must uphold the law even now*!

So instead, as if the whole world could read our intentions coupled with the guilt of maybe being caught in the act by a distraught owner, I was quickly brought to my senses and I jumped out of the van without hesitation, finding that it wasn't necessary to start directing the children.

"Any luck kids? Spot anyone?" I exclaimed.

We all instinctively started to look around and beyond, with the hope that the owner was knocking about somewhere close. Maybe they had stopped to chat with a fellow dog walker and this little beauty had wandered off.

Maybe.

Meanwhile, I believe love at first sight had just happened between Lucy and this beautiful dog.

Our four legged friend stood perfectly still and quiet as Lucy bent down calmly with her dainty hands disappearing in the swathe of shiny black and white fur on its back, from its neck down to its tail, back and forth in a swooshing fashion, her head right up against the dog's face and whispering something into her sticky out ear.

In grateful response, the dog didn't move a muscle, blink an eyelash or twitch a whisker. It just licked the back of Lucy's hand when she ended her message.

Its huge amber eyes focused and gentle.

# CHAPTER 7

# DON'T LEAVE ME

"God only knows what all that was about!" commented Lucy's mum, Kathy, who had been spying on the drama from her front seat window.

"And it's a *she* dog," commented Matt.

"Oh, I guessed that already, Matt!" Lucy responded. How utterly adorable…" squealed Lucy.

I heard that comment loud and clear and it prompted Kathy to turn around to catch my surprise, too.

We didn't murmur a peep. Both our eyebrows just lifted in unison. As far as we knew, Lucy had only ever known a male Bendog!

*I guess it was just a matter of elimination, my dear Jack!*

Realising that the owners may be actually losing their mind over their missing dog - I knew that one! Had read the book, bought the t-shirt and was wishing he or she would turn up this instant and claim this adorable doggie.

"The point is", I tried to enlighten the children, "there are sadly many stray dogs roaming the streets here on the Costas where we holiday. And thankfully, many British animal charities, who try to tackle this problem, are inundated with stray dogs. They do what they can with the resources available but, inevitably, some have to be put to sleep if they can't be rehomed."

With mention of the dreaded *sleep* word, in unison, they all let out a unanimous "*OOOOOH NOOOOO!*"

So we all made a decision.

Matt offered his observations first.

"Well...", he said –

*Graaaact*! Matt cleared his throat .... "um... eh... sorry about that...errr...OK!" Matt was ready. "She is sporting a newish red collar and although it doesn't have contact number nor a name inscribed on the metal identity part, her owners may have just bought it for her and haven't had the time to get it engraved. Errr...something like that", he added.

Lucy spoke next, her feet *tap..tap..*tapping on the pavement as she danced from one leg to another, in eagerness to participate and offer her findings.

"I find our lovely little fur ball in very good health. She has a glossy coat and her ribs don't stick out, so she's not too thin. I conclude that she is being well fed! BUT!" – she pulled down her dress hem, bowed her head, and quietly added "I don't want to lose her. I love her already! There. That's all!"

And with that statement sorted, Lucy lifted her head, automatically bringing her bushy bunches to immediate attention by the side of her ears.

Matt moved over to the passenger window so he could speak directly to his mother.

"What about you, mum?", asked Matt, "what do you think we should do?"

"Well", said Kathy in reply, her arms folded over the open window frame, her head turned to the right. She was leaning as far out as possible to look at both of her children and then up and down at the precious creature.

"How on this earth could such a beautiful loving creature like this one possibly be a stray? It would be hard to believe she doesn't belong to a loving home somewhere. That's what I think.

And therefore I think we will have to leave her here for her owners to find her, which they will very soon. I am sure of it!"

I bobbed my head up and down like a nodding dog in agreement with Kathy. We wanted to give this little mite a chance.

Her best option was for us to leave her in the vicinity she found us and hope she would either find her own way home or be reunited with her owner. I had to sadly abandon this dog on the pavement and live with my conscience for the hereafter.

Not an easy decision.

# CHAPTER 8

# LUCY'S HEARTBREAK

Time was moving fast and I just had to accept that I was going to be late for choir. After all, I had a decent excuse to offer Roger, didn't I? Well, yes, in my world, but I doubted - knowing Roger's code of punctuality and team accountability- that in reality he wouldn't see the sentiment in the same way. However, I decided on the spot that it was worth taking his wrath.

I turned the engine back on.

"We must go, I'm afraid. The dog obviously belongs to someone local – ", was my best effort of reassurance. I tried hard not to care.

As Matt, then Lucy - with deliberate slowness - clambered back into the warming machine, I was hailed a lot of *buts* and *what ifs*, some of which had good reasoning behind them.

"What if we just borrowed her whilst we are on holiday and looked after her?", searched Lucy.

"Lucy, that would be theft… She's someone's pet, not ours", replied Matt.

"But I really miss our Bendog… and… she's so much like him", insisted Lucy.

"How do you think *your* Nan, back at the Villa, would react if we just showed up with a stray dog?" Kathy questioned them.

"Ummmm, not sure..." said Matt, sitting up quickly and paying attention to the latest question. Appearing more fidgety, pulling down the ends of his shorts towards his knees at the very thought of the outcome of that scenario. His Nan was a tough talking Irish woman with a huge warm and giving heart…but maybe not that big as to welcome our new four legged friend here in Spain.

After all she was still too worried about Bendog.

Meanwhile, Lucy continued to converse with herself. Mutterings were abundant.

"Nan would be fine about it, I'm sure. If only she could see the poor little darling… she would want to help it. I just know she would", she murmured to herself, audible enough that I could just about make out her sentences. That was the way she dealt with her feelings. "And I'm sure the owner will be out bellowing for it as soon as we have gone," I replied as confident as I could.

Through the wonky rear view mirror - yes, another inherited contraption from the previous owner - I just caught sight of Lucy. She was knelt upon the back seat, her face pressed against the back window with her hand stretched against the window pane.

Her fingers, from thumb to little finger, one by one slowly and reluctantly waving to the lonely stray. I couldn't quite see Matt's position due to the wonky mirror, but Kathy informed me that he was sitting with his head down, staring at the floor, fiddling with his hands.

"Sorry kids…", added Kathy.

As my foot hit the accelerator, I focused on the road ahead.

Soon we were heading north towards our destination. We were already twenty minutes late. Our minds were trying very hard to concentrate on the day's activities ahead of us. But Lucy in particular was unusually very quiet the entire journey to the beach.

Of course I was subjected to a blow by blow commentary from Matt as to the position of the dog, which turned out to be of one clear observation. The beautiful creature had remained in the same spot, her head tilted to the side and her gentle amber eyes focused on our departure, until we were out of sight.

"Oh boy, I really thought Bendog had turned up. Crazy, eh? He's on my mind a lot." I confided in Kathy. She nodded her head and replied.

"It's a difficult time for all of us…" Kathy projected as she turned towards me and squeezed my arm. "That's the attraction with this stray dog, Jack. She seems so familiar."

*Um*, I mused, *too familiar maybe!*

# CHAPTER 9

# THE CUCKOO'S LAST STAND

"Brrrrrrr, this Irish weather, it's got suddenly freezing in here! Can you feel a draught?" I moaned to Nan, rubbing my arms, trying to warm myself up.

"Lucky for you sittin' there in yer fancy Donegal wool coat!" I laughed.

Nan, sitting in the passenger seat pushed her head up from the large collar like an emerging turtle coming up for air.

"You must have a window open or something, can you check?"

Nan shuffled about within the tweedy wool coat, trying to turn to her left. But the stiffness of the wool slowed her movements to a near stop. It would have been easier for me to stretch across and check for myself.

"Oh", I said… "not so fancy now, eh?"

Nan didn't reply, but responded with her nose in the air and her eyebrows lifted, desperately pulling the wool over her exposed knees with her free hand at the same time using her other hand to check up and down the wet window pane.

Finally she spoke.

"Well, it's not dis side" she replied, "it must be yer side." Nan nodded her head towards my window with a wry smile appearing slowly.

I squirmed about as much as one can, whilst keeping my eyes on the road. I felt the window pane from top to bottom.

"Nope, it's not here either!"

*Something is causing it somewhere*, I queried to myself.

And I drove on.

We had only travelled about three kilometres from the cottage. It was 3 a.m. on deep bleak March night. Still wintery in temperature, with heavy rain. All we could hear were the *schwump, schwump, schwump, schump* of the car windscreen wipers.

"Thank goodness those are workin good. It's lashin wit der rain!", exclaimed Nan.

"No lovely moonlight tonight to accompany us on our way along this narrow rambling back road!"

I was on my way to the airport in Knock West Ireland. Nan and my beloved fourteen year old Bendog were dropping me off for the 6 a.m. flight. And as per usual, we are both tired, having gone to bed and then laid there awake. Well, at least I had.

Listening for the cuckoo to *cuckoooooo* twice…as it sprung out of the wall clock at 2 a.m. If it wasn't for the loud snorting and snoring emanating from the upper bedroom, I may have believed Nan hadn't slept a wink either!

"I don't know why we put ourselves tru all dis. Dat Gerry Ryan fella is raking it in. 'Ere we ar' in da' middle of da' nite, lashin wit da' rain, stressed ooout, on a fifty minute journey bur' will take probably two hours. I mean, just to save a few bob on Ryan Air! We must be demented!"

"I know, I know. It never seems so bad when you're booking a flight. It's just that we never seem to remember how we felt about our last early morning departure. We've not one good memory between us." Nan and I both laughed.

"And that damn cuckoo on the wall", I moaned to Nan, half-heartedly. "Now I know why Paddy Magee took the law into his own hands! If I'd had the means at 2 a.m. this morning I would have done it too!"

It is said that Paddy Magee, the previous owner of the cottage we now lived in, once fell on bad ground with a fellow in the pub below.

He was so mad that when he returned home full of *poiten*, a very strong drink made from brewing malt, barley, treacle and potato skins, he bade down in his chair mumbling inaudibly to himself by the dwindling turf fire and quickly fell into a deep slumber. Dead silence fell upon the room only for the sound of Paddy's deep breathing that rattled like brittle iron train wheels on an old track, as his chest lifted and fell.

And as the dawn light peeped into the kitchen through the open window, Paddy was suddenly wakened by the sound of the cuckoo who had made its appearance as usual at 5 a.m.

*Cuckooooo! Cockooooo*! It sang out at the top of its voice.

Only on that particular morning, Paddy Magee was, in no way, good humoured. Still wildly emerged in the excess liquor and enraged from the night's events, Magee jumped up from the low handmade chair.

*Glup! Glup!* His knee high leather boots soaked with wet mud, strolled across the stone cold flag floor. He reached out with one arm and grabbed his large double barrelled shot gun that was leaning against the fire hearth. He padded his feet to the ground, like a runner about to surge forward at the start line of a race. His wobbly large muscular quads twitching, straining to keep him upright. He was a big stout man. Fearsome looking to some. His deep dark eyes set back into his head against his wilting weather worn leathery skin, covered in overgrown stubble.

And yet, apparently a deeply caring and sensitive soul who loved his animals - and normally an upstanding good catholic - Magee lifted the gun slowly from the ground. Never moving his head. He brought the gun to his eye level and aimed it at the clock.

As the cuckoo sung his fifth *"cuck...ooooo"*, which unknown to him was his last and final one...

*BANG! BANG!*

Two shots it took and the clock was blown off the wall.

*Schhp,,clonk,,szsinglez.bzzzzup!* The cuckoo's home, springs and all, blasted into smithereens all over the kitchen floor.

"Ahhhhgg", cried Paddy Magee as he steadied his weapon against the fire hearth. "That'l take the cuckooooing out o' yuuu!", Magee shouted at the top of his voice.

After that, he promptly collapsed back into his low chair by the cold fireside and was away with the fairies and snoring in seconds.

All of this account told by his young nephew who lived with him in the small wee cottage. They never did find the remains of the small cuckoo bird.

I like to imagine it looked down the barrel of the gun and sprung forward through the open kitchen window milliseconds before Paddy Magee pulled that trigger.

"Ah, yes...." said Nan, "the cuckoo clock... now that's a rare and expensive heirloom, Jack! I'm very pleased I've still got me-own, given to me on Mother's day back in 1974...", she remarked. "And don't yer go batterin or hokin and poking it, de yer hear me? It does no wrong on me, I hardly hear it att'all. Att'all!"

"Yes, I know," I chuckled to myself.

"It's Mother's day today, Jack!", reminded Nan, bustling her chest forward and lifting her chin high in the air. "Trust me t'b in der wrong country t' get me flowers!"

My lips stretched out into a sly grin. Unknown to Nan, I'd been tipped off by her family that she'd get her delivery later that day.

But I kept my mouth zipped.

# CHAPTER 10

# MISSING

Nan and I met in London in 1996 and since then we became good friends. Both with nursing backgrounds, we shared a common goal of owning and running a Care Home and, within a few years, we had pooled our money and bought a small one in Kent. It was successful but awful hard work. And the long hours soon took their toll.

From the profits, we bought a small Irish cottage and renovated it with the help of Nan's eight grandchildren, who visited during their holidays.

As soon as I met Nan, she welcomed me into her family. I guess I offered her companionship and support in raising and entertaining all her offspring. And I looked upon her as my big sister who was very good at keeping me grounded. We shared many interests together and we loved our exciting travels in our motorhome.

"Did yer close the back door of t' da van when we left?" asked Nan, as she turned her neck around to check. "B'jesus!" Nan cried, "the winds howling tru!"

"Of course, I did! Oh My God!" I shrieked as I checked my rear mirror. I could see through the van to the back door and the reflection of the tail lights shone brightly as I pressed the brakes.

*I shouldn't be seeing those from inside the van,* I thought to myself, immediately realizing that the only reason why I was seeing the lights was because the back door was… wide open!

*SCREEEEECH. Bumph*! I abruptly pulled over on the side.

"The back door is open!" I screeched to Nan.

My heart sank into my stomach at that moment. I instinctively knew something was very wrong. I clambered out of the door and ran to the back of the van.

"Ben, Ben!", I called into the back. I couldn't believe how dark and suddenly unfamiliar it was. I couldn't see a hand in front of me. I called loudly the dog again.

"Here boy!" I quickly stepped into the cold back of the van, my mind repeating *he can't have got out….how…but how? When… but when?*

"Ben, where are you boy?" I moved swiftly around in the dark. My hands outstretched like a zombie, blindly searching along the seats, hoping to suddenly be upon his warm fur.

Nan could hear the panic in my voice and she was making her way around to see for herself.

"He's not here!", I cried.

I felt a hot rise in my throat. An overwhelming feeling of nausea. My heart was beating fast against my chest wall.

"B'jesus! He must be!", replied Nan as she squeezed past me, going further down into the recesses of the van. "Old boy! Will yer come out dis minute!"

We were both waving our arms and hands across the seats and feeling along the floor as if we were imitating the hokey cokey! It was a nightmare from hell, those few minutes of realizing that he was… missing!

"Ben, Ben …here boy!" cried Nan and I in turn, then both together. Our voices breaking, tearful.

"Ben! Ben….dog….here… boy! Come on boy, where… are… you?" My words were shaky and inaudible through my broken sobs.

Outside I hollered as loud as possible, out into the wild.

*"BBBBBBBBEEEEEEENNNNNN!"*

# CHAPTER 11

# THE SERPENT TAKES HOLD

I didn't care who I woke up.

Although that was unlikely to happen, as most of the houses were well off the road side. The thought of my nearly blind, almost deaf old pal out there in the dark wet cold air, lost or maybe injured…

I just wanted to scream.

My heart was taking a beating I'd never experienced before and I could feel my head pulse thumping against my temple.

Quickly recalling to each other the events that night, me and Nan concluded that Bendog must have got out just after I had put him in the van, just before I locked up the cottage.

So Nan and I back tailed home, fully convinced that Bendog would be waiting at the gate when we pulled up.

But, as we pulled in at the drive ….there was no one to greet us. He was not home or anywhere to be found.

We decided to search around the house.

"Ben! Ben!" we called.

"Bendog….come boy!" We called in and out of the byers…. "Here boy!"

But it brought no joy.

The tension steadily grew in my body as if a large snake had taken hold at my feet and was crawling inch by inch, circulating my legs, tightening its grip slowly and surely.

My mind raced, searching for answers. The lashing rain had pitter pattered so much. It ran like a frightened river down my hair and spread across my neck, cold, just like the slimy snake that was squeezing the life out of me.

I beckoned to Nan to get back into the van and to head up and down the route we had been driven along. With her new plastic knees showing their worth at last, she was inside the van in a jiffy.

The rain drops hit the windows.

*Flick a flack fleck* sounds all around us.

The urge to drive fast was unbearable. But I couldn't. What if we drove past him? Or even worse: what if we still drove into him?

Oh My God! So many thoughts…my emotions…the snake's grasp.. squeezing… *Urggg.*

" 'Slow down Jack. Keep her steady…Jack!" , cried out Nan.

We drove a little further down the road, right of the cottage, but we changed our minds and decided to stick to the original plan.

The cold blooded reptile had arrived nearly at my throat, and I didn't see the deep ditch behind as I turned the van around.

Suddenly the van jolted back.

*GGKDUMMMPT*! I wasn't in reverse…*What the*... ????

The white front bonnet had lifted off the ground. And we were both looking up at it.

"Mother o' God, what was dat?", screamed out Nan.

I quickly wound down the window. The back wheels spinning in mid-air.

*VWPP... VWPP... VWPP*... Over and over.

And the van balancing over the ditch!

# CHAPTER 12

# TRAPPED!

"Oh no!" I cried to Nan, "I don't believe it! We've bogged, and we're hanging over a big ditch, trapped! This night can't get any worse! What about my boy?"

Tightly the reptile wrapped itself around my entire body, my mind emptied and my breath drew shorter gasps for air. The urge to just collapse into my seat was so very tempting…

"Just get a grip, Jack! We've got to get out o' here furst, somehow!" yelled Nan.

We were both aware that any sudden movement could be catastrophic.

With not a soul about at that time of the night, coupled with our state of minds, it made the situation much worse.

I understood why the body cuts out given an overload to deal with. Mine was at the edge….but for Nan… I couldn't think straight at all. I was panicking. My heart was thumping in my chest, my hands were sweaty and sticky, and my mouth was as dry as a bone.

Nan kept saying "It'll be alright Jack! It'll be alright." Her words seemed so far away… I knew I just had to pull myself together and pretty sharpish.

Although Nan was trying to keep me calm, I knew that she was like a duck. Calm, floating about on top of the water, but the legs going like mad underneath!

I carefully pushed the driver door with all my strength. It was heavy and hanging at an angle with gravity definitely not on my side.

I only needed enough space to get out. I slowly lifted my right leg, bent at the knee and carefully jammed it between the door and the car chassis.

*QCECECKREEKK!* The van jerked slightly.

“Take yer time, Jack”, Nan cried out at me, crossing herself quickly and calling out Holy God and the Mother of Christ, as she always did when needing help from above.

I pulled myself up with both arms holding onto the roof edge. I squeezed my body out of the car and held onto the door frame whilst Nan maneuverer herself to keep the balance.

*PHEW! What a relief to be on the outside…*

But now Nan? I can only imagine she was cursing her new Donegal Wool coat, although I’d never say it to her and she would never admit it. It was going to prove a hinder, a nuisance at this moment. I was sure of it.

“Ok, look, eh... you need to balance the van somehow so that it won’t tip!” said Nan, no longer a spring chicken nor a size fourteen.

Five children, and eight grandchildren later gave her more than enough reason to taste her family’s home cooking and indulge in the odd bars of chocolate. Suffice to say she was of stoutly proportions, yet able to touch her toes without any effort, much to the amazement of her granddaughters!

“Don’t yer tink I know dat yer eedjit ye… I flean down on der bonnet Jack, put all yer weight on it, I’ll try and shift meeself over onto yer seat.”

I knew from old that Nan knew best, no point in trying to argue. No. We’ll do it her way. I’m happy with that.

I gently lowered myself onto the farthest corner of the bonnet. I didn't even feel the wet cold metal against my body, with enough vision to keep my eye on her inside the vehicle.

"OK! DO YOUR THING!" I cried out to Nan, my voice shaky, imagining my nerve endings fraying into pieces.

With small precise movements, Nan shuffled herself around, stopping after each one until she was facing the driver's seat. Her lips were so tightly pressed together, showing a determination so fierce it would surely scare a wild wolf. Her eyes were fixed and focused on each destination she had to reach. I had imagined she would have put her leg across the driver's seat…but no, not Nan.

*SQUEEEEKEEEK...PLLLONNTTT!* Some sort of metal gave out a cry and the van tipped gently and silently back and forth before coming to its own halt.

"AAGHUUFF!" Nan cried out.

"Are you OK?" I shouted. I could still see her shape upright through the windscreen.

"I…I am….goin te' lie down across the seats, I tink it will be the best way to steady it", she replied bravely and within a minute she had disappeared from my view.

I have to admit it looked as if the tweed wool was acting like a slip mat that enabled her to turn more easily without too much force. Amazing! How she did that I'll never know. So brave!

Anyway, I didn't care about the damage to the van in that moment. I just wanted us to get out of that new mess in one piece.

"Go you and wake up Mick", she ordered me "and be quick. Mick can pull us out wit his tractor!"

"NO! Never! I can't leave you here!" I replied.

*Got to get a grip girl...got to get help girl...come on now...*My eyes closed. *God give me strength.*

And in a moment of respite, I felt calm and in control enough to ignore the snake's grip.

"OK!" I screamed back at Nan, and I slowly slid down the bonnet onto the wet boggy ground, away from the van. With Nan still in it!

Oh! What a decision! *Damned if I do and damned if I don't.* My nerves kicked in again. It was back, the suffocating viper. Worse than ever.

"JUST BLOODY DO IT!" I cried out into the deep night.

I knew deep down it was our only chance of recovery.

"Go, I won't move a muscle, I promise!" Nan said bravely.

I was away up the road, like a whippet after a hare. Luckily our good neighbours only lived eight hundred yards away and with the surge of adrenaline pumping around my body, I suddenly found myself outside the bungalow.

*BANG! BANG!* On their bedroom window.

*BANG BANG!*

"MICK!" I cried, "It's me, Jack!We've bogged the van and its hanging over a huge ditch! Nan's still inside and it's about to tip right over! Bendog's missing too!" I pressed my head against the window while I hammered it. "It's a nightmare! Can you help please?"

Mick opened the window and I told him again of our plight!

"B'Jesus!" he said. "I'll be right out!"

Theresa, his missus, came running out into the yard.

"Go and jump on the tractor, Jack!" she shouted through the sheets of rain, her neat little nightdress soaking up the dire wet unwavering weather.

And before I knew it, Mick had started up the tractor, and we were on our way down to Nan. The relief of hearing the rattle and roar of the tractor's engine en route to Nan, lifted my spirits enough to scare off that vile venoumous viper.

It was no problem for Mick to be out in the night. He'd often be called to help with new births amongst his cattle or help a neighbour with a difficult one. He was used to pulling huge beasts out of ditches.

Mick attached the tow rope to the van with Nan in it and pulled her out without a bit o' fuss or bother in the world.

We couldn't thank him enough, and whilst we watched him take the big blue machine back home, we had re-grouped and were focusing on our next move in the drama to find Bendog.

Slowly but surely, we continued with our mission. Time was of the essence that we didn't think about our near catastrophe.

We drove the van, stopping at intervals with the windows down.

"BEN…BEN…WHERE ARE YOU?" We kept the engine ticking over, as we waited for a sign.

We searched for hours, up and down the road, until we were so exhausted we decided to go back home, get some sleep and start again early the next morning.

After a few hours of restless tossing and turning, we were back on the road.

The daylight was just on its way as we headed down to the spot where we had encountered the incident of the open door. No Bendog! I turned to Nan at some point.

"It's madness I know, but do you think the dog heard us talking about… you know… going off? It just seems weird that the back door flung open, and we can't find him."

"Dat dog knew everything you tought or did before you even tought it yerself, that's what I tink, so I'm not surprised he's missing now!" said Nan, as soft as she could put it to me in my highly charged emotional state, her eyes narrowing in a suspecting manner.

Needless to say, I missed my flight and two weeks' work in Devon! I just couldn't leave my dog out there. I just wouldn't!

Naturally with his eyesight being poor, his hearing pretty bad and his heart not that great either, I knew he wouldn't be fit for a long trek home anymore. Even if his nose was on the right scent. The thought of him lying somewhere, perhaps vulnerable, cold and frightened, maybe injured, hurt my already saddened heart.

Those feelings were always a reminder that the slippery slimy snake was not far away, waiting to pounce, unannounced. And that I would never have any peace until my boy was home again.

I just wanted to find my boy and bring him home.

# CHAPTER 13

# MOTHERS DAY SADNESS

*KNOCK! KNOCK!* I banged on my neighbour's doors and windows, on the local houses and farms along the route and waited until someone answered.

No one had seen or heard him.

"He even had his red lead attached", I'd say to each of the neighbours, speaking in a slow drawling kind of way, disbelieving at each door that no one had seen or heard anything.

The feeling of worry, my shoulders hunched over, my head low, not really wanting to face another disappointment. Deep sorrow clung to my heart as the day went on.

And still no Bendog.

As time went by over the next day, still no sightings of him reported here in this part of rural West of Ireland.

Despite putting up notices, I contacted our local radio station. His name seemed too bound out of the local radio on the mantle.

*"A black and white springer spaniel of nearly fifteen years, called Bendog is thought to have gone missing around the Ballymote area last evening. He is wearing a red collar and still has his red lead attached".* Read the reporter. *"Please call the following number if ye have any information."*

It had been obvious from the outset, that the main obstacles hindering our search for my beloved pet was the thick undergrowth, deep ditches and large boggy areas that hugged the roadside, making it difficult to search thoroughly.

I realized too, that if he had got his lead caught on a thick branch, he wouldn't be able to untie himself and could be lying in a ditch somewhere.

I was torturing myself with imaginative scenarios, and as time went by, the outcomes of these seemed to become less and less positive. At some point I just wanted him home. Alive or dead.

If he was not alive, at least I could bury him in his beloved bog-garden, so I could be near him every day. He had been such a great friend and the thought of any future without him in my life was cutting me in two.

Nan was much more optimistic.

"Aw now, he'll 'ave been picked up by some aul farmer and be lying by a cozy fire in a wee cottage on the mountain." she said cheerfully. "Dats it, dats wher ee'l be!"

I returned a quick but half-hearted smile, hoping and praying that she'd be right.

But I wasn't so sure. Somewhere inside of me, I knew this might be the end. Bendog had gone missing and I might not set eyes on him ever again or hold his lovely face in my hand, smell his wet boggy coat after a day *frogging*. His generation had come to an end.

But still, I left an outside light on.

*Just in case.*

# CHAPTER 14

# I CAN TALK DOG

By midday, here on the Costas the sun had made its mark. Clear blue skies and hot sun!

Lucy, Matt and their mum had all had a smashing time at the beach. And from the amount of *beach* shaken and sprinkled across the back seats I would be surprised if any was left for the remaining sun worshipers!

I had quietly manoeuvred my way into the back row of the choir unnoticed and out of sight of Roger. He was up there lost in directing anyway and sadly my voice unnoticed by its absence too! Oh well…C'est la vie!

Heading back to our nicely air-conditioned Villa was a wonderful image. That is if the children's Nan had remembered to switch it on!

It wouldn't be the first time we'd arrive back from an outing and she'd be sitting in the shade on the terrace, happy as Larry, drinking a fresh hot cup of tea and the house as an oven inside.

Soon we'd all have had a good dip in the pool, cooled off, if only to warm up as soon as we stepped out of it. This time of the day, the pool still remained at least six degrees colder than the outside temp, which by now was about twenty eight degrees and rising.

No need for towels, no extra washing!

“Nearly home now!”, I shouted across my shoulder to anyone that would be listening. I glanced into the larger than normal rear mirror, which offered a more or less panoramic view of activity in the living area of my Ford campervan.

I saw Lucy with her nose and hands up against the side window in anticipation of seeing her four legged friend.

“Oh, she’s been at that window since we turned off the main drag”, mumbled Matt. He had obviously moved on and was probably planning how to execute his new underwater *Jaws* manoeuvres once in the pool.

“Yes, you’re right Matt, but it’s because I whispered in her ear that we wouldn’t be long and she was to wait here until we came back!”, Lucy replied.

We pulled into our usual spot and I switched off the engine.

“Oh no! She’s not here!”, cried Lucy eager to jump ship, both hands grasping the door handle as we pulled into our parking spot. She was the first one out onto the pavement, her head turning so quickly from the right to the left scanning like an anxious bird. I thought it might suddenly whizz completely around and take off into the air.

Her legs of eight years growth were twitching as if she was standing on hot coals. Her mouth drawn down, her shoulders hunched, a slow disappointed look appearing on her face as it dawned upon her loving heart that her new friend had gone, and was nowhere to be seen.

‘‘Come on Lucy”, called Matt, “you surely didn’t think she’d stay in that same spot for all the time we were at the beach, did you?”

“I love that dog and she loves me too. I can talk dog. I know her,” she cried as she sought solace under the arm of her mother, who stretched out her free arm and pulled her close.

“I know,” said Kathy, “she was very special but I’m sure she’s ok and back with those that care for her, ok?”

Lucy nodded slowly, tilting her chin down and frowning, her lips pressed tight. As she untangled herself from her mother's arms, she exclaimed in a hardly audible voice.

"I'll have to tell Nan all about her, won't I, mum?" and with that she set off on a brisk business- like walk, arms folded heading towards the top of our street.

Matt was following behind, dragging the sandy beach bag, swinging it from side to side like a pendulum in a clock.

"Hey Matt!" cried out his mum, "steady with that bag!"

As I circulated the van, locking all the doors one by one - *no central locking on this little eighteen year old diamond*! - I too peered around as far as my eyes could see, just in case I spotted a black and white furry animal.

*A love at first sight... hmm, very unusual to be so short lived,* I thought as I followed the pack home, my mind on the inside of the fridge and a cold San Miguel beer with my name on it awaiting my attention...*lubbly jubbly*!

We were all in single line as we approached the top of the street, hot and bothered. Kathy was looking back at me and we were giving each other that shame-she's-very-disappointed-eh? look.

"Should we have lunch first or jump into the pool?" I asked to lighten the mood.

"POOL !!!" everyone cried in unison.

"Yes!" shouted Kathy.

Suddenly Lucy, who had just turned the corner ahead, screeched at the top of her voice and for all in Benidorm to hear.

"She's here! It's her! She came back and she... she's here! She's here! She's at OUR gate!"

# CHAPTER 15

# BENDOG'S GRAN'DOG'THER?

Lucy was so excited that as she turned to tell us her great news, her left sandal remained pointed downwards and her foot had swung towards the rest of us.

I have to confess it comes from her Nan buying her sandals two sizes too big.

" 'Aw now…twill give hor feet more room to grow, B'Jesus!" exclaimed Nan whenever confronted over buying for Lucy! Typical rationale from Granny!

Meanwhile, Matt saw this as his chance to abandon the bag mid-trek and hotfoot it down to the gate, leaving me the only one with hands free to stuff all that had spilled out back into the bag and bring it home. It wasn't long before Lucy suddenly *had a moment* and screamed back up the street.

"How did she know this was our gate? There are thirteen other gates in this street!" Lucy cried out.

"Oh! That's not rocket science, Lucy", said Matt in-between patting and acquainting himself with the new arrival.

"She must have smelt Nan's cooking. Well, I don't blame her. Nan's a real good cook and I bet this dog is going to love her cooking too. Just you wait and see."

"I knew she'd find me! I knew she would!" cried Lucy, hopping around the gate. The little dog head stretched up, never once taking her eyes of the hopping girl.

Caught up in Lucy's excitement - and I have to admit somewhat relieved, myself - Kathy and I stepped up the pace until we reached the commotion at the gate.

As sure as eggs are eggs, there she was, in all her black and white glory, this little sweet treasure, tail wagging vigorously, her small hips trying to keep up with the pace of it.

Eager to pat the dog myself, I suddenly became aware that all of this sudden squealing and liveliness may have been too much to bear for our street neighbours. Most don't get up until the afternoon, while others have probably just settled into their siesta, a wonderful Spanish tradition fully embraced by the ex-pat community. Our street was made up of mainly retirees.

I had visions of rotten Spanish tomatoes hurtling towards our party from the various terraces above and beyond! On that thought, I quickly herded my flock in through the gate, spilling out into the tiled garden. Dog and all.

In all of the commotion we had all forgotten how close we had become to self-combusting as the heat was mighty, and that our plan to take a cool plunge before lunch had gone right out of the window. It was 2 p.m. and the hottest time of the day.

"Take cover under the gazebo!" I cried to the welcoming committee. "Bring the dog too, Lucy. Come on, Matt."

Matt had taken a towel from the beach bag and was hovering it over his head, trying to get the shade from the streaming hot sun.

"Oh – that's a great relief!", he cried, as he swiftly joined us under the gazebo and instantly dropped the towel onto the tiles.

Nan, who was preparing a wonderful fresh *buffet* of wonderful Spanish cuisine had been sharply interrupted from her *tapas* creations. The children wouldn't eat any of them, although the hot dog and pan - a French stick in Spanish - was nearly always on the menu for them.

Whilst she had been concentrating on getting the prawn's tails all facing the same way on the plate, Nan had heard a noise outside the kitchen door and scurried out onto the terrace that reigned over the garden area.

"What''s occurring out here, b'Jesus? You'll wake the neighbours!"

"Nan, Nan! Look! We found a dog! She's beautiful, isn't she? She's like a little Bendog! And she loves me! Do you think it's his gran'DOG'ghter, Nan?", laughed Lucy, her eyebrows raised, her eyes as big as saucers, waiting expectantly for Nan's opinion. Nan leaned over the railings to get a better look and as she spoke, the little dog's head lifted up and its hind legs automatically shifted into the sitting position.

"Aw well, she is a pretty one arl roight and very like auld Ben too, but what is it doing here?"

In true Matt fashion, he replied.

"Nan, it's simply your cooking she could smell, you know what dogs think. Lucy, really!" At that, Matt left our company and ran into the house to grab the key for the pool gate.

"Well," said Lucy, crouching down and hugging the canine to her neck, "we met her near the van this morning. She was alone wandering around. We were just about to leave when Matt and I jumped out and petted her soft fur and she licked my hand. Matt discovered she was wearing a collar, so mum and Jack said she must belong to someone in the area. But Jack was going to be late for choir practice so we had to leave her." Lucy paused, shaking her head. "It was terrible Nan... What if someone had done that to Bendog and left him alone and homeless?" The corners of Lucy's mouth drooped quickly, her shoulders rounded.

She stared at the ground for a moment, as if to hide her sad thoughts of her lonely Bendog.

"Well, she looked lost and helpless, too. And I thought about her all the time we were at the beach".

Well, that would be a sincere enough comment all right, knowing how caring and thoughtful this dear child is and how upset she felt about Bendog's disappearance.

*It wouldn't surprise me that having fun at the beach would not have wholly distracted her from the welfare of her new friend*, I thought to myself.

Lucy let go of the dog's neck, stood up, jumped three of the six steps and was at her Nan's side in a tick.

She continued her tale. "When we got back from the beach, she was nowhere to be found, and I was very sad, Nan. I thought I would never see her again. EVER! And I raced ahead to come and tell you of my sorry tale when I turned into our street and saw her sitting by OUR gate."

Kathy, who was busy emptying the beach bag and was organizing the wet swimwear on the plastic sun-dryer, turned her head towards Nan.

"Yes Mum, that's about right, although she is wearing a collar", Kathy stated "And it looks in good condition."

"It's a red one. Looks new", piped up Matt.

"I just can't believe she's here!" said Lucy, looking directly at Matt. "I knew she understood me. See Matt, I do know what dogs think." Lucy promptly jumped back down the steps, pulled back an ear of the dog to expose the collar for Nan to see.

" 'Is der a name on the collar?" asked Nan.

"No," said Lucy, "but I'm going to call her Lilly."

"Hold on, pet. She isn't our dog!", I called over.

"But she's here now and her name is Lilly!" exclaimed an excitable Lucy.

I knew there would be no point arguing at this stage as to the future of this pet. Lucy was now more certain than ever that this *Lilly* was destined to her keeping forevermore. She had cried so much over Bendog's disappearance! I didn't have the heart to stop her flow of love for this one.

"Get her some water, somebody", called out Nan who's eyebrows raised up as she studied Kathy's and my next move, "she must be parched!"

"We don't know how long she's been on the road. Maybe she's hungry too," called Matt through the balustrade on his way to the pool.

Lucy fetched some cool water from the fridge and poured it into a rather nice salad bowl that Nan was fond of, only to be promptly sent back into the kitchen to exchange it for a chipped one from the end cupboard.

"We'll have to go to the supermarket and get some dog food" I said, directing my statement to Lucy, who was kneeling down next to the dog, watching how she was lapping the water so fast it was seeping out of the side of its gums!

"I think I'll take Lucy and Lilly up the road to the supermarket when its sundowner time, around 5.30. It'll be cooler then and there should be a few locals out and about, maybe call in at the local bar, stay a while, have a coffee, get water for the dog and a juice for Lucy. That way someone may recognise her", I confided in Nan and Kathy who were setting the table.

They both nodded in agreement.

"You'd better tell Lucy of your plan", said Kathy, whose natural instinct thought it was best to prepare Lucy just in case we had to hand over the dog there and then.

"Um, let's have a dip first ok? We soooo deserve it!"

Pauline Edmunds

# CHAPTER 16

# A FAMILY FIESTA

"Back in a short while," I called to Nan who was rattling about in the kitchen.

"Don't let Lilly out!" called Lucy.

Unknown to us, Nan returned from the kitchen, called the dog up to the terrace and put some fresh chicken onto the cool tile for her. Needless to say, she wolfed it down, drank a little water and gently lay down outside the front door. She was going nowhere.

It wasn't too long before we were all sitting on the shady terrace, having enjoyed our quick dip.

We were enjoying another magnificent feast of good local produce. There was a luscious green salad, sliced beef tomatoes with olive oil and crumbled feta cheese. On the left, an amazing Spanish tortilla, still warm from the oven. On the right, a delicious tapas creation made of crab meat, mayo, carrot and a designer platter of fresh whole prawns, all arranged around the bed of mango, pineapple and melon slices. To complete the banquet, a bowl of ever popular *aioli* - a delicious Spanish garlic and mayo dip - and a fresh *pan* cut into one inch bits, laid in a wicker basket.

And last but not least, to help it all along, a chilled bottle of *vino blanco* for the adults and orange juice for the children.

As we all tucked in, *oohing* and *aaahing* at the variety of flavors, Lilly stretched herself out, feet under the table, quiet and content as if she had been with our family forever.

Sitting here on the terrace, admiring the clear blue skies, chomping away at this mellifluous spread, dog at my feet, it felt just like the old days.

It was times like these I pondered. *Maybe buying this off plan bargain Villa looking at how we were all so sun-kissed and happy, wasn't all in vain after all.*

# CHAPTER 17

# ALL CRIED OUT

After ten days of no good news, with a terribly heavy heart and newly bereaved facial expression that was to accompany me on my journey - full of sadness and hopelessness - back to England, I boarded the flight.

As the plane soared over the Emerald Isle, all the lovely shades of green fields and countryside brought me no comfort on this journey. In fact, quite the opposite.

It was a stark reminder that I was leaving my best beloved boy out there, lost somewhere in similar fields, most probably alone, cold and fretful. It was unbearable.

I turned away from the window, slumped into the seat, my shoulders aching from my heavy sobs. Unaware of anyone around me, I ploughed myself into the jacket I was using as a pillow and sobbed and sobbed. My diaphragm sore from trying to conceal movements of my heaving chest.

So much sadness and guilt, I just couldn't help myself.

Arriving back at my job was harder than I imagined as all who knew Bendog during his many stays over the three years, were eager to hear the sad tale but offering sympathy and hope only resulted in bursting into moments of tearful sobs.

I kept thinking *what am I doing back here? I need to be out there looking for him!*

At least Nan was still at the cottage and I felt calmer and reassured by that image. It was a comforting thought. Even though her optimistic outlook of positive scenarios, despite being cheerful and hopeful, didn't fool me one inch!

I knew it was all for my benefit, bless her.

I kept thinking back over this past week, that I had seen her on a few occasions, standing in the kitchen in the middle of the night, just staring into his bed, a damp hanky in her hand.

It said enough to me to know that her deepest fears were being realized too.

It got to the point that I could not talk about him to anyone.

Until one day, when I was out walking with a friend, I saw him. I really DID! My eyes opened like large in amazement and I really did! He was running around the park wagging his tale, head down and sniffing madly.

"Dear God! I cried out loud "IT'S HIM!".

My heart flipped over.

"I'm sure".

I could feel a rush of heat from my toes enveloping my entire body and I was about to start calling him, when my friend kindly took my hand, pointed to its owner.

"I'm sorry, dear. It's not Bendog…".

"Oh no", I cried drowning my head into my hands, the tears flowing like a waterfall. I just couldn't control my emotions.

Many times in these early days I'd be driving somewhere, when suddenly I'd see him on the pavement or across the road. And before I knew it, I'd have the window down, and started scanning for a place to park, calling out to him the whole time.

Those dogs just kept their head forward, not even looking up.

Eventually, as painful as it was, I had to accept it was never or ever going to be my dear Bendog.

There is, sometimes, no rationale involved in the grieving process. After all, how could he be here in Devon - for goodness sake - when I'd left him in Ireland? But it was my natural instinct to believe every black and white Springer Spaniel was HIM.

I *needed him* to be alive, even if it was just to say a final goodbye and bury him in his own plot with all his belongings in his beloved bog-garden.

I do feel strongly that it's every person's right to be awarded respect and the time to heal through the grief delivered over losing someone they loved very deeply. Whether human or animal.

As Khalil Gibran once wrote on his book *The Prophet*,

*When you are joyous, look deep into your heart,*
*and you shall find it is only that which has given you*
*sorrow that is giving you joy.*
*When you are sorrowful, look again in your heart,*
*and you shall see that, in truth,*
*you are weeping for that which has been your joy.*

And he was so right.

# CHAPTER 18

# THE HOOLIGAN THAT NEVER GREW UP

In between the dark, gloomy days of grieving for my little chap Bendog, I found myself becoming preoccupied with the good memories of him. You know, the ones that made me laugh and gave me that perfect feeling of joy… and the ones that would make my heart sing and make me smile at seeing him in great form, running, sniffing, and endless retrieving.

Even into his golden years he'd make us roar with laughter. In particular the sausage attack! That became his party piece.

We would give him a string of sausages and he'd take one end and throw it about and around in a lasso fashion. And then he would instantly drop the sausages to the floor, hoping he'd manage to free at least one from the string that was holding them together. He'd growl at them all on the floor when he realized his plan hadn't worked. And he'd just keep on going until he freed one, then another, then another. Until all the sausages were lying on the floor!

Oh! Bendog had brought such much pleasure in his long life and I was grateful for all of that joy and unconditional loyalty and love he showered us with.

One time, we had stopped off at a gorgeous beach on a visit to the North West coast of the Emerald Isle. I believe they made *The Blue Lagoon* film there many moons ago. It was just two of us and the dog. Nan and myself stretched out on the golden sand on that lovely sunny day, with Bendog lying quietly next to us. He too used to enjoy the sun. And with not another soul in sight for miles, we soaked up the rays.

We must have nodded off because when we woke up and looked about us, Bendog had surrounded us with newly dug deep holes in a complete circle. It was hilarious! He was very industrious that day, in fact. I wondered if we hadn't woken when we did, we might have fallen into the hugely dug hole which was now the size of a crater!

Nan's family used to visit us on the coast particularly during the summer months. Nan would prepare a large picnic and eight of her grandchildren would turn up at the same time. All the girls would be in their bathing costumes, if you can call two bits of material a costume!

Anyway, they'd be lying sunbathing and the boys usually splashed about in the sea. Bendog, too. When the dog had had enough, he would come out of the water and walk right up to where the girls were lying. Then he would walk-in between them and stand quiet until one of them screeched at his presence.

Then he would go for it, shaking his body so vigorously that all the sandy sea water dispersed onto the three bodies either side of him. The screams and curses from the victims would make your hair turn white!

It was only hilarious if you weren't caught in the spray. Otherwise, IT'S NOT FUNNY, NAN!

That's the hooligan part of the dog that we loved so much. What a character!

There is, of course, one story I just have to share with you and that's how I came to own the little darling in the first place. And that's a real TAIL! I mean tale!

# CHAPTER 19

# THE BEST CHRISTMAS PRESENT EVER!

It was Christmas day, 1996. We had only moved into our new home in July of that same year. The large Edwardian house had been a residential home for the elderly and entering it on completion day, it was like the remains on the *Marie Celeste*.

All the tables were laid for dinner, cups upside down on the saucers, knives and forks and napkins. All so neat and pristine. Even the beds were made up, ready for occupation.

Nan and I looked at each other. It was, to be honest, quite unnerving and a bit weird, but the general excitement got the better of us and it wasn't long before we were renovating and upgrading.

That particular Christmas day, we had invited my father and my stepmom, my brother, his wife and their three young children. We had also coming over Nan's son with his family of five young children, including two sets of twins. So it was going to be a great day for all.

Everyone had arrived and dinner was to be served in a wonderful dining room with its long oak table and plenty of chairs covered in newly stitched *skins* in an oyster satin material. Very posh and all designed by Nan.

I had used the lovely high walls as a blank canvas. I had stencilled a beautiful collection of Roman pillars upholding planters either side of the cast iron fireplace, with a variety of flowers overflowing from them. They were much admired by my guests, and I was very pleased with the effects myself.

The children were highly excitable and kept running up and down the circling staircase along the landing and in and out of the thirteen bedrooms. I had noticed though, that they made numerous attempts to whisper, in turn, into Nan's ears, and then they would run away back up the stairs.

As I caught them at this malarkey, I banished them from the kitchen one by one for bothering Nan, as she was obviously busy preparing Christmas lunch. And the turkey still had to have its *socks on.*

"Jack!" called out my nephew Damien, "Have you any music we can put on?"

"Well, err, yes. But I have it on in the sitting room", I replied, knowing full well I didn't want the loud party effect.

"What about out here in the hall or dining area? A radio perhaps, just for the fun, eh?", insisted Damien.

I remember that at the time I thought it was a rather odd request, as we were just about to eat lunch. And the foreseeable chatter I was certain, would generate enough noise as it was.

I didn't want to appear *bah-humbug* on Christmas day. So, despite being under the - mental as well as physical - pressure of serving fourteen guests, I quickly hunted out and handed my nephew the portable radio. Without any hesitation, he immediately plugged it into the wall socket nearest to the table and switched it on, turning the volume to the highest level.

Much so, I'm sure the flowers started vibrating!

"Oiy lad", I said, "turn it down a bit, ok?"

"Ok, Jack, sorry. I'll leave it here on the hall table!"

"Fine!" I said.

And I went on with the business of opening the special Christmas day wine, one of my more favourable responsibilities of having guests: *Chablis 1990.*

After lunch, whilst I was helping with the washing up, I was summoned into the dining room by my brother.

"Come on Jack! You have to come NOW!" called my brother, advertising a most unusual grin across his face. And I thought I knew all of his expressions! This one baffled me as I dried my hands on a nearby towel, his hand gesturing me into the room.

As I entered the room, everyone was standing around the cleared and nearly empty table, save for the red festive candles and a large newly covered and decorated cake, mainly with grubby little finger marks.

All that work for days we've been at it and now, in a flash, it was all over... *Oh well, never mind.*

*It is superb. All of it,* I was thinking, when the younger children pulled me by my arms and the older ones started pushing me from behind towards the fireplace, shouting,

"LOOK! LOOK!" Their little fingers pointing towards the large grate in the centre of the fireplace.

"Santa Claus left you a present!"

As I stretched my neck above the children's heads, I could see a small purple bag. It looked like it was made of velvet, soft and squishy. Only this one seemed to be moving about in the fire grate.

"What on earth...?", I cried, as I knelt down in front of a moving object. Suddenly, I could hear whimpering too. The wriggling continued and the noise was coming from the bag.

"Open it, Jack!" cried the children in unison.

"Ok, Ok!" I said. I could feel a thousand eyes watching as I slowly untied the yellow cord.

As I finally opened the top of the bag, out popped the most beautiful black and white head of a puppy, whimpering and crying as I unravelled its little body and lifted it out of the fireplace.

"Oh, how wonderful...he's beautiful!" I cried.

I sniffed that unmistakable puppy smell to a round of applause that nearly lifted the roof, as everyone clapped and cheered this new arrival into the family.

"Thank you so much, Santa!" I exclaimed, looking over to the window. For the children's sake I had to make believe he was out there, having just delivered his package down the chimney.

Of course, I knew it was a gift from Nan. How she had kept it a secret, I'll never know because I had had absolutely no idea at all. It was the greatest surprise to me!

"It's a wonderful present. Best ever!" I cried to the children who were each trying to tell me their version of what had been going on behind my back since the pup's arrival early that morning.

Unknown to me, Nan and nine year old Damien, went very early in the morning together to pick him from a litter of pups at a nearby farm. They had ordered him six weeks prior, so he'd be ready for collection today. Damien, aware that I was a Newcastle supporter, picked out the black and white one. Nan had sanctioned his choice and they returned straight away, before I was up and about.

According to Nan, throughout the morning, the children were given the task of keeping the puppy away from my ears and so they had decided to keep it upstairs in one of the rooms far enough away.

Its whimpering and crying could be heard apparently by anyone walking from the hall to the dining room, which of course, would have mainly been me as I was in charge of the table preparations.

Yes, now it all made sense. What I had thought to be - I have to admit - somewhat strange shenanigans of children's activities on a Christmas morning, were to make perfect sense after all.

The whisperings to Nan, the need for the radio, the running up and down the stairs all morning, the children running up to me, smiling and running off again, for no reason. That was all part of the plan.

Seeing the funny side too, it must have been excruciatingly difficult, especially for the younger children to keep this wonderful secret and not let the cat, or in this case the dog, out of the bag!

Although, I guess, I would have forgiven them for almost anything as I held this small delightful bundle of fur in my hands. A Springer Spaniel, a breed I'd longed for since I can remember.

I loved him from that moment on and will love him forevermore. His name was Benson, soon to be renamed Bendog by the youngest toddler.

It was to be the best Christmas present ever!

*It's so true*, I thought, *there hasn't been a better one since.*

# CHAPTER 20

# OUR PLAN

‘"Eh! Hands above the table, please kids! It’s not a good idea for Lilly, the dog, be begging at a table. Especially giving her bad habits. She obviously doesn’t do it at home.”

“Wherever that is…” piped up Matt.

All this time, our new visitor had remained lying prone and didn’t seem to want to annoy those above her.

“B’Jesus”, said Nan, “she’s not like that hooligan Bendog, is she? He couldn’t stay still for one minute, sniffin and lickin anyting and everyting in sight! m’Lord…aarlright!"

“Yeah, but what a character!” I said in his defence.

I missed his presence in my life enormously and never knowing what had happened to him would haunt my heart forever.

Then again, looking at this little one nearly the spit of him, I couldn’t help thinking that divine intervention had maybe had a hand in this situation and brought her into our lives to help us grieve our loss and watch over us. As Bendog had for so long. And, of course, there is the slight possibility that she could indeed be related to old Bendog, but it was hard to prove now. Wouldn’t that be a miracle? God I’d be delighted.

But of course it wasn’t over yet.

I stood up from the table, plates of empty prawn tails and wilted lettuce to clear shouting to Lucy that the time had come to see if we could find her real owner. I tried to sound nonchalant and unperturbed as if we were returning a borrowed cup of sugar to a neighbour.

"Oh no, really?" Cried Lucy, "can't she stay here with us now? Look how happy she is! Please! Please let her stay…" as she twirled her scooter around on the spot like a helicopter blade.

"Lucy!" called Nan as she patted the chair next to her, "come err. I want yer."

Lucy dropped the scooter and jumped the six steps and plonked herself onto the saved seat.

"Imagine", she said to Lucy, keeping eye contact and holding her hand. "If someone like us had picked up Bendog when he went missing and decided to just keep him witout a taut as to how the owner's family would be feeling. Remember how upset you and Jack were? How we all were and still are? Each and every one of us was very concerned for Ben's welfare. We were all worried and anxious. So, darlin, we 'ave to do der right ting, and do you know what dat is?"

"Yes, I do know Nan! Bu...t, she loves being with us…ME!". She stood up abruptly, the sides of her mouth started to droop, her eyes watery and narrow. Her brother put his arm around her shoulders and with words of ten year old wisdom…

"Its…err… the right thing to do, Lucy".

Lucy made no reply. She took the tissue from her dress pocket and blew her nose into it.

"So, here's der plan", said Nan. "You and Jack take Lilly up der supermarket café bar and sit outside. You have a drink, chat to Mario, Consuelo - you know dat crowd up der - and wait and see if anyone has any information or recognises hor."

Lucy bent down to pat the visitor and said in a whispered secret. She thought we couldn't hear anything.

"Don't worry, Lilly. You and I know you are meant to be with us. But we must try and find your real owner cos they will be very worried by now".

Meanwhile, I was hunting around in the shed outside and came across a lead we used for Bendog when we used to take him on his walk.

God he didn't like the heat! We'd have to wait until around ten at night or very early morning so he could have his sniff. I held it in my hand for a few moments, stroking the worn patchy leather strap. My mind sifting through the countless memories and re-feeling the feelings of pure joy he had brought.

Once he heard CLICK, the sound of his lead being separated from his collar. He knew his freedom had arrived.

And now I was attaching it to another dog.

Mixed feelings? You bet!

# CHAPTER 21

# SO FAR SO GOOD

We all settled down for a lazy after lunch sunbather siesta, each finding our own favourite part of the terrace, roof solarium or a shady place amongst the vibrant bougainvillea, native here in Spain.

Oh! So many lovely colours!

There was a light to dark pink, a goldy, yellowy, one rosie red, deep red and - my favourite of all - the splendid lilac to purple.

All out at the same time of the year, mind you, much to the annoyance of our neighbours, the petals would fall off in the autumn and because of their lightness, almost paper thin.

They accumulated in and around the corners of the wall enclosing the swimming pool. When we were not in residence, someone else had to sweep them up! Not to mention the very hard branches and extremely hard spikes that could take your eye out if they caught you at the wrong moment. Or if you weren't looking where you were going!

A flower of such beauty needed such fierce protection! I am in no doubt about that!

Lilly had found her spot too, under the table on the terrace, where it was cool and quiet.

“Such a lovely quiet dog,” remarked Nan from the couch in the lounge, “what a lovely pet to have.”

It was about 5.45 p.m. and as I took the last slurp from my iced mint tea, I called Lucy.

“Let's go,” I shouted across the garden. “Put the lead on the dog. It’s cool enough for our walk, you know where?”

Lucy bent down and stroked Lilly’s head, feeling for her collar, and as she attached the lead, she whispered something into her ear.

"Don’t worry Lilly,” she said quietly, “I really hope no one claims you. We can keep you then, but that's between me and you, ok?"

As if the dog understood what was being said, she licked Lucy’s hand in response and both made their way to the gate.

To my surprise, there wasn’t as many people at the bar cafe as I had imagined.

We took a seat at the table near the entrance under a large Coca Cola umbrella and ordered our drinks. Our table was a good vantage point for all those coming in. We must have stayed about an hour, maybe more, and spoke to anyone passing introducing the dog and appealing for information.

Even Mario and Consuelo, the owners didn’t recognise her. And they knew everyone.

“She’s not from around here. I’m sure,” said Mario as he bent his six feet physical frame in half, in order to give Lilly a pat on the head.

“Oh, she’s so lovely,” said Consuelo in her rather attractive spanglish accent. It was her parents who owned the cafe and a huge new modern villa behind.

She kindly offered Lilly a bit of salami from the counter, which she swallowed whole at once.

*Slurp*, *slurp*, her wet tongue swiping from one corner of her mouth to the other savouring any trace of her tasty treat.

*Why is that?* I had often wondered. *Why do dogs in my experience swallow a piece of good meat in one gulp, no chewing, no savouring, just... gone?* And yet give it a piece of toast or remnants of a biscuit, and they seem to chew it until the cows come home? Beats me!

I soon realised that we were not getting very far. In fact, Lucy was far from disappointed that no-one had come forward. She sat there with a big grin across her face when I said we should return home.

I decided to take the longer way back. The sun was still quite high in the sky and the oppressive heat was now slowing down. It was pleasant and more bearable.

"Can we go past the peacock cage on the way home, please Jack?" cried Lucy.

"Don't see why not," I replied, "we'll pass it on the way."

"Yippee!!!" shouted Lucy. "You'll like them too, Lilly." And she skipped off in front, dog at her heels.

# CHAPTER 22

# PERKY PEACOCKS

At the top of the road, behind the supermarket, stood two enormous villas, each surrounded by the mighty fine walled gardens and massive gates. *Very imposing indeed,* I thought.

I believed them to belong to a wealthy Spanish family who owned the land that urbanisation was constructed upon. They also owned three peacocks who resided in a man-made large cage across from these mighty gates. They also owned a rather large Alsatian dog, who luckily for us - not him - was kept tied up alongside his shelter to guard, in case there would be any intruders that might take a fancy to these rare birds.

We crossed the road to get a closer look at the creatures, when, suddenly, we heard an almighty howl and squawking coming from the cage.

Lilly immediately started to growl at the birds as all three peacocks at the same time opened their tails and displayed their magnificent coloured feathers, squawking incessantly in a high pitched squeal, strutting around the cage as cabaret show girls in floor length coats of feathers.

Lucy, her mouth open, froze on the spot, her eyes full of wonder and awe. She stared at these spectacular birds as if she was hypnotised.

"There's all shades of greens, blues, purple and golds!" she cried.

"Oh, so beautiful! I've been up here before, but they have never opened their wings like this before. Yes! Yes! They really are perky peacocks!"

"Yes, they sure are", I replied.

"And look at the female hen! She's so dowdy and unassuming by comparison."

"Sooooo AWSOME!" cried Lucy and she continued to be the perfect audience for these show-offs.

I sensed Lilly was frightened, so I pulled the lead off Lucy to take better control, just in case she bolted off.

Meanwhile, the guard dog had pulled himself up in a casual manner and made his way over to the fence. *He must be used to all this show,* I thought. He seemed so laid back and calm.

Still, I didn't quite trust him enough to offer my hand through the wire, unlike Lilly, who seemed to be taking an interest in the big dog as she also had her nose up against the wire.

I convinced Lucy to leave the birds and speak to him, whilst I moved Lilly away from the dog. But as we past closer to the birds, I felt a strain on the lead.

Lilly started growing and barking at the birds again in-between, swallowing hard, her amber eyes as big as saucers, a sure sign the dog was feeling very threatened.

*Poor little thing*, I thought. And I quickly crossed over the road. Lilly didn't care much for this show and she was giving as much as she could back towards the cage, her neck straining to get the last bark in.

"Well", I remarked to Lucy, "this little madam can certainly stand her ground! Good on you Lilly!" and I patted her head.

Mind you, I'd had enough of the noise, too. It was deafening!

"Right! Let's get home", I said, "Better get back to mum and Nan otherwise they'll be wondering if we were lost too, not just silly Lilly".

"She's not silly, Jack! She's cute and a little timid, that's all", said Lucy.

On the way back, Lucy and I discussed Lilly's reaction to the birds.

"I want to be a vet!" stated Lucy, "I just adore animals. All of them." She paused. "Well, except spiders. I hate them!"

*Of course!* I thought for a second and the penny dropped. *Of course! The vets!* The dog might be micro chipped! *YES!* And if it was registered, it should show the address of the owners.

It would mean going down to the vet in the village that exact same night! They were open till 9 p.m. Well, I felt it was worth a try!

And I discussed my idea with the family, indoors, as soon as we arrived home.

# Lost Treasure

# CHAPTER 23

# FANCY DRESS

Nan and Kathy said that they could hear our voices as we returned from our walk. They were for us waiting on the terrace. I could see their eyes eagerly peeping through the balustrades to see if they could see whether Lilly was still with us.

Lucy eagerly greeted them, her voice high pitched and elated.

"Oh yeah! Mum! Nan! No-one knew her! And Mario and Consuelo said it was unlikely that she was from around here, cos' they'd know." Lucy looked around. "Where's Matt, mum? I must tell him our news!"

A voice from the pool area shouted across.

"I'm here Lucy! Is Lilly still with you?" Matt had spotted us walking past.

"Of course she is", Lucy replied, "I told you! It's magic!"

"Oh! That's great! See you in a minute," said Matt. I could just make him out through the gate, clambering out of the water, his over-sized diving goggles in his hand.

From the broad smiles on the faces of the two home birds, I could tell Nan and Kathy were also relieved, but we didn't want to raise too many hopes just yet.

'I've been thinking…What if we take Lilly to the vet tonight before we go for a walk along the village for an ice cream? Could we go early"?

"Why the vets?" asked Kathy.

"Yes, were you tinkin microchip, Jack?" asked Nan, nodding her head in agreement.

"Yes! I replied. "No harm, eh? Just got to do it, you know? Wouldn't feel right just keeping her, without trying to find her owner".

"Ok, dat's settled", said Nan. "We'll all get dressed up, take Lilly to the vet and go on from der to the village and at the same time, someone might recognize her."

Lucy called Nan into the bedroom and said she wanted to wear her Spanish dress and her new red shoes to go with it. Nan - of course - agreed and started helping Lucy into her costume.

"We'll put yer hair up, like a real Flamenco dancer. What about you Matt? Do you want to be a Matador?"

"Not likely", replied Matt, "I'm fine the way I am, thanks Nan."

And he disappeared very quickly, before Nan had him washed, dressed and in full bull-fighting costume, equipped with a spear and a red flag!

"What about Lilly, Nan? Can we dress her too? She'd look so cute."

" I don't tink der vet would find dat funny, do you? But I tell you wat I'll do. I'll bring a piece of red spotted material I got from der market with me and make hor a wee skirt. Then we'll stop at the Chinese supermarket on der way and pick up a lovely sombrero, more appropriate for a Spanish dog, Ok?"

"Ok!" cried Lucy, "Oh Nan, you're the best!" And she made her way out to tell Lilly, who was lying in her favourite spot under the table.

It didn't take long before we were all dressed to the nines for a night out.

First call: the Veterinary Clinic, downtown.

# CHAPTER 24

# LUCY'S DESPAIR

It was a lovely warm summer evening.

And the scent of the Frangipani bush in the garden accompanied us to the end of the street.

Lucy looked wonderful in her costume, her hair in a bun, like Nan promised. She could have easily been mistaken for a Spanish señorita.

"She has such good posture for wearing clothes", her mum discussed with us on our walk.

Matt was in his - no, not orange shorts - but in his new three quarters length *bermudas* and a plain short sleeved Ben Sherman shirt. *Very cool looking*, I thought.

I raced him along the way.

Lucy's red shoes were traditional flamenco ones, with a heel too.

"I bet those shoes won't stay on for the whole evening. She's hobbling a bit now," I confided in Nan.

"Not t' worry, I've put her soft plimsolls in me bag!" Nan whispered.

As we all approached the vets, I felt a pull on the lead. Lilly was trying to turn around her little body to go back.

"Lucy! Pick Lilly up, please. She's obviously nervous about going in here", I cried remembering all too well how Bendog would stop dead in the road as soon as he caught a sniff of any clinic. He would not budge one bit. I had to pick him up, as heavy as he was, and carry him in.

Bendog hated the vet. Any vet, ever since his first visit as a pup.

That time, a vet had hurt his back during an examination and from then on we dreaded taking him in. It looked as if Lilly may have encountered the same fate. I know some people who feel that way about the dentist. Thankfully, I'm not one of them!

The lady vet came out from behind her desk, and Lucy put Lilly on the tiled floor, bending down herself to keep Lilly company. I explained the dog's circumstances and the vet went to get the gun to prove if she was wearing a microchip or not.

There was one under the skin in her neck. The vet matched it up with her computer.

"Yez, zsee is microcheeped. Correcto!", said the vet. Then she proceeded to explain. "Lilly is fifetine monts olde", she declared with her spanglish accent. "Lilly waze rescued by a dog charitty az a puppy and she waze plaicede with a famileey in zer villarge", she explained.

And, according to the vet with the funny accent, it seemed like Lilly was up to date with all her jabs and in good health.

An absolute silence invaded the nice vet's room.

Not one of our party reacted. We just stood there. So the vet continued. Lucky for us she spoke very good English.

"Zee haz a famileey in zer villarge, but I don't 'ave an address. I do ave a noomber for zer charitty who wescued er, a ladiees aname, I could give you? Zat's all I can do! Ok?"

We thanked the vet, took the number, and were making our way out of the double doors, when…

"Señorita!" she called, looking at Lucy, "para muy bueno!" No need for translation. We all knew what she had said to Lucy.

"Gracias.", said Lucy, embarrassed.

"Hey, that was a compliment coming from a real Spanish lady, eh Lucy?" said Matt. Lucy smiled in recognition, smoothed down her red spotted dress with all the frills and she followed with Lilly to the van.

Nan broke the silence.

"Let's go onto the village. We need cheering up, eh? Who's for a big ice cream?" called Nan, at which Matt jumped up and punched the sky."

"Yes", he cried out, "it'll be a mint choc chip for me!"

Lucy was trailing behind with Lilly at her heels. The dog looked up at her every ten or so steps, as if to say, *hey, what's happening, you've gone all quiet*! Lilly wasn't the only one to notice the sudden mood change in Lucy.

"You're quiet, darling," said her mum, as she waited for her to catch up.

"I was so sure, mum, that Lilly would be with us forever…" Lucy said, trying hard to hold back her tears. "I can't give her up now. I love her and she loves me… I just can't mum… I just can't."

Kathy was about to console her daughter when Nan sensing the child's distress, called her to her side.

"I know child, I know. We are all feeling sad, we all have mixed feelings for Lilly's future…"

"ALL except Matt!" howled Lucy, working herself up into a state, pulling at her dress, tears streaming down her red cheeks.

"But we have to follow the details the vet gave us. We can't be selfish. Her real family will be worried", continued Matt, "don't you think? Just following doc's orders, Lucy!"

"Well," she cried out, "if she had SUCH good home as you all think she must have come from, how come she's so happy with US, ME, in particular? Maybe, just maybe, she ran away for a good reason, or got lost… or whatever!"

Lucy was so upset, indignant and defensive; I really didn't know what to say. Some of what she had said *did* make sense. After all, the dog was of a nervous disposition. If you came upon her suddenly, she was very nervous and her little body would start to tremble. I hadn't noticed it until now. And she cowered, her tail tight between her back legs at any loud noise or sudden movements.

Maybe Lucy was right, but it was not for us to judge.

At least not yet. Not until we meet the owner. And even then, there was nothing we could do if they did, in fact, claim her.

Slowly, but surely, the fate of this lovely little lady was going to be taken out of our hands sooner than we thought. And I had - we all had - become very fond of her. We wouldn't want to have to give her up to, what we would call an undesirable owner.

As we are all too well aware, there are far too many of those in the world.

# CHAPTER 25

# SPANISH EYES

"Nan!" cried Lucy, "what about Lilly's dress?"

"Ok, bring hor over to der van in a minute!"

Before long, Lilly appeared, sporting a small frilly elasticated skirt made of the same Spanish material as Lucy's - red with white polka dots - and a small *sombrero*, also red with spots, on top of her head. It was a little bit too big, perhaps, but Nan attached an elastic strap that went under Lilly's chin and it was more secure.

I shook my head in wonder. *Another of Nan's impromptu inventions,* I thought. She'd do anything for these children! Lilly just stood to attention, like a real model would!

"You'll definitely have plenty of Spanish eyes looking at you tonight, ladies!" I said, trying hard to sound up-beat.

Lucy took Lilly's lead and both walked off as proud as Punch. What a lovely sight too. Kathy and Matt walked on ahead, giving me time to call the number of the lady at the Rescue Centre.

"Oh, I see", I said, "thank you!"

"Wcll?" said Nan, who'd stayed behind, eagerly awaiting my news.

I told Nan that the lady, who seemed very nice, said she did indeed remember this pup, as it was one of six. She had placed it with a large growing family of four small toddlers and another one on the way. Their mother and father lived in a flat in the village.

"Unfortunately she couldn't give me a recent address" I explained. The lady had been made aware that the family had moved from there just after placement.

"So, we are no further forward", replied Nan to my news. "We may as well go into the village and have a drink anyway, seeing as we are here", Nan suggested.

It was a busy Friday evening in the village square, with its newly laid grey tiles. The local Friday evening market held along a side street, just off the square, was in full swing. There were stalls with colourful fruit and vegetables. Stalls with colossal amounts of differently flavoured olives, swimming in barrels of garlic cloves, chillies and onions. There was fresh *jamón* - ham in Spanish - which was cut as you waited off the large leg bone and also a gorgeous fresh fish stall with an abundance of fish and seafood.

And a queue to match.

Nan and I discussed the tiles as we walked over them, both concluding that, of all the beautiful coloured tiles made here in Spain, this council opted for plain old grey ones.

"Unbelievable!"

There was a fountain and a statue of Our Lady in the middle and plenty of hustle and bustle from local Spanish families chatting. Children were running around playing games on the tiles and the usual expat residents were sitting outside the many watering holes dotted around the newly laid square, enjoying the same.

A very normal summer evening, one which we loved to walk down to, drink the local brew. Sometimes buy supper and do some *people watching*. It was a pastime you could indulge in throughout the year, not just in the summer months.

As Lucy and Lilly paraded around, bringing many smiles and pointing fingers from the many Spanish eyes watching this pretty spectacle, Matt chose a table with a large umbrella and five hard plastic chairs facing the square.

Drinks were served as well as whopping ice creams and Lucy seemed brighter now that she realized we had hit a dead end and we didn't know where Lilly lived. And that meant she would be coming home with us. *Hurray*!

"Water for the dog, too?" asked the waitress as she put a clean ashtray full of water on the ground.

Lilly found a spot further in and she was crouched down between my legs, away from the edge of the square. *Probably quieter for her*, I guessed. And she remained there for the remainder of our stay, resisting any further calls from Lucy to be shown off to her newly acquired temporary friends.

Indulging in the warm evening glow and atmosphere of what attracted us to coming on holiday to the Costa Brava in the first place, I resisted the temptation to further down another pint of San Miguel beer. Instead, I opted for a brandy coffee, a specialty called *La Bomba*, made of Spanish brandy and hot chocolate, a delicious bed time tipple.

It was getting late and Nan was yawning. It was time to make a move. Lucy and Matt were somewhere swallowed up in the middle of the square, coming back and forth to take a sip from their drinks.

"Five minutes kids!" Kathy shouted.

We had decided to take a slow stroll home and we were organizing our departure, when suddenly two boys of about nine and eleven years old approached our table.

The blond haired boy in a yellow T-shirt spoke first and in good English.

"Missus?" he said, looking straight at Nan and then at the dog, who was right at the back of the table, hardly visible from the edge.

"We know who that dog belongs to."

# CHAPTER 26

# GOOD NEWS??

That's my phone ringing, I thought as I hunted the usual places I may have put it.

I didn't like to take personal calls during the day at my work, unless they were important. And the only thing important to me since Mother's day was my missing boy, Bendog. So, when I saw the Irish number flash up on my mobile, I grabbed it immediately. I pressed the green light and heard Nan's voice on the other end sounding quite upbeat.

"Jack!" She said, "I ad a visitor come t' me door tis morning! He had heard I'd lost a dog!"

"Yes! Yes! AND..?" I cried down the phone, my voice sounding both panicked and excited. I daren't think of the outcome of this conversation.

"Well now, he says he tinks a dog matching Bendog's description is being looked after buy an elderly woman. Dey call der goaty woman, on account that she keeps goats up and over Potash Mountain, at the back of the first turning in der road. She lives in a caravan and has loads of dogs too."

I've lived in Ireland for thirteen years now and I still smile at the way the locals give directions. My heart and soul met somewhere in the middle of my chest and tears welled in my eyes.

"Oh, sweet Lord! Let it be him," I cried down the phone into Nan's ears.

"I know, I know. I'll drive up der as soon as I've me socks and shoes on", said Nan. She too was excited and hopeful, I could tell by her raised voice.

"Ok, GO!" I shouted. "Let me know as soon as!"

I put the phone inside my bra, so I would know exactly where it was when Nan rang back. I could hardly contain myself.

*Oh Bendog, is it you my precious boy? Are you sitting at the feet of the old woman in front of a cosy fireside, being fed little tit-bits from her worn and wrinkled hand? God, I hope so.*

Oh, I had so many scenarios running around my head since that call. Some of hope, some of…well I didn't want to think on the negative, but these thoughts were tormenting me so much, I just had to share them with my boss and his ninety nine year old mother. They too were glowing with hope! And naturally they kept asking me if I'd had a call.

As the hours passed by and still no word, my heart sank further and further into my boots. I couldn't concentrate on anything and kept checking my phone just in case I'd missed a call.

Surely Nan would have rung straight away if it was him. She knows I would be anxiously waiting. *Maybe she can't get a signal, maybe she can't get an answer at the door...*

There are some folk who live out in the rural harsh landscape of Eire that wouldn't trust any car approaching their abode, let alone one with an English registration. However knowing Nan as well as I did, I was sure that her Taurean determination would not be easily ignored, especially on such an important mission.

# CHAPTER 27

# THE OLD GOATY WOMAN

When the phone eventually did ring, much later than I had expected that day, it nearly gave me a heart attack. The ringtone rang out against my chest as I fumbled between my layers of clothing, dropping it onto the cushion nearby in the panic to answer.

"Well, what happened, is it him?" I exclaimed.

"Em…em…well", said Nan in a low tone, reminiscent of her quiet friendly counselling conversations on the phone.

"What do you mean, eh…em? Was it Bendog or not?"

I could hardly keep my cool. The suspense was drowning me. Of all the answers I had mulled over in my mind, this scenario was definitely not on my list!

Nan proceeded to give me the blow by blow account of her mission.

"Well" she said, "I drove up and around the mountain until I came across der caravan. We've passed it before, when we took our goat Shamus back up into der hills. I got out of der van. There were goats of different colours, sizes and breeds all around the caravan. I knocked on the door and waited, and waited. Eventually a little lady bent over from aging osteoporosis wit hor hair tied in a neat bun at the back of hor head, she stared at me wit one of doe's suspicious looks in her eye, pulled the door ajar enough so she could see my face.

*Top o'der mornin, what der ye' want ere?* she said to me. I knew I wouldn't be gettin in for a drop o' tea anyway", Nan continued. "I smiled and told her the tale of Bendog. *No, no, he's not ere. I've enough dogs of me own*, she said. I asked if I could take a look at hor dogs, I know it was rude of me not believing hor, but I wanted t'be sure as she seemed a little too keen to get rid of' me. *If ye must*, she said, and when she pulled the door back and about, five or six dogs came running out, nearly knocking me over in the rush for the yard!"

And Nan continued her saga.

"Up until that moment, I was feeling quite optimistic, but oh dear, I looked at each one in turn, none of them were our Bendog. One was similar in colour, but not him. I'm sorry Jack, I wanted to cry there and then." Nan's voice quivering with emotion.

"I was so disappointed and I knew you'd be too. And the kids…".

The two of us cried down the phone, each trying to comfort each other in between the sobs with the one-liners. *It's going to be ok, it's not your fault, we'll find him...*

At least I knew that our neighbours and locals would be on the lookout for the dog as he still had his lead attached.

But as the days passed into weeks and not a word of any sightings, my hope started to fade.

I started to collect his toys, his holiday bed and food bowls around my workplace to take home to Ireland. If nothing else, they would in time bring comfort to me. I was sure of that.

Sometimes having hope does bring peace and joy. And that's wonderful.

But when it doesn't, the feelings are painful, raw and deep, almost serving to protect your heart from ever wanting to deeply love anything ever again.

# CHAPTER 28

# LILLY GETS A NEW NAME

One of the boys ran off across the square, leaving the other one at our table. But in two ticks, he was back again accompanied by a dark haired boy, very Spanish in his looks and of about the same age.

Matt, who had up until then been engrossed in a football game, bolted over to the table calling Lucy, who was talking with a bunch of girls. Lucy appeared within seconds and she was very interested in why we were talking with those boys.

"It's his dog, Missus," said the blond haired boy in the yellow t-shirt.

Lucy defiantly caught hold of Lilly's lead and proclaimed that they would have to prove it! Her little face was twisting, fighting back the tears.

"Ok!", said the Spanish boy.

"Come with us and I'll take you to where we live. You can ask my mother!" And with that announcement, we all trotted off behind the boys.

"It'll be better if we see where she actually lives", advised Nan to Lucy.

Lucy, ignoring Nan's plan, and without replying, marched along with Lilly, who was frantically trying to keep up. But her four little legs hardly had time to touch the ground.

"I'd better go in the front", I said to Kathy and Matt. "You two keep track of this route. We might just need it later."

I don't know why I said that. After all, it looked like a *fete-a complit*. Why would we need to come back?

This was it! Bye-bye Lilly.

I just dreaded the journey home…

The boys stopped outside of the front door and pressed the doorbell. It wasn't long before a very young looking woman opened the door and stepped out onto the pavement, giving the Spanish boy what seemed like a telling off - only in Spanish -.

When she calmed down, the boy explained what had happened in the square.

"Oh Milly, you've come home", said the woman, taking the lead from Lucy's hand. "You are a naughty girl, Milly!"

Lucy took hold of Nan's hand and mine, as we stood in the street. Looking through the door from my angle, I could see clearly. Four partly clothed, nearly naked toddlers, about a year apart, each standing on a step of his own.

It was a sight to behold, I must say!

I glanced at Nan and motioned the scene just with my eyes. She moved her feet to get a good look too. Her raised eyebrows stayed in one position long enough for me to know she was as flabbergasted as I was.

"Oh!", said Lucy to the woman, "did you call her Milly? Is that her real name? I have been calling her Lilly!" continued Lucy, letting go of our hands to rub and pat Lilly - or Milly- , who instinctively licked her hand.

"Well", replied the woman, "Milly ran away. Must be a week now. That's right, isn't it Pablo?"

"Yes, mum", he replied.

*Quite a sullen boy*, I thought. He didn't seem in the least excited that the dog had been found. Neither did the mother.

I got the feeling she was just going through the motions, pretending to be elated.

Lilly didn't seem very pleased either, her tail under her legs, no wagging. She just stood there, next to the woman. With Lucy trying desperately to reassure Lilly, gently patting and stroking her, I noticed she was swallowing hard too. She was so anxious, poor girl.

Nan piped up. "She's been with us only a day."

"She hasn't been reported missing, either", interrupted Lucy. "And we've been to the vets, too!" I suppose she was trying to make her point that it was the least they could have done seeing as she was missing for a week.

"Ok, Lucy." said Nan taking her hand.

I took hold of Lucy's other hand and gave a gentle squeeze.

"We thought that if no one claimed her - and because there was no address on the microchip - we would keep her for ourselves. You can see she would have been well loved." I explained to the mother who was busy shooing her brood back up the stairs.

Matt stepped forward.

"You see", he said, "our old family dog went missing in Ireland on Mother's day this year and we've never found him. And the thing is, well, Milly, I mean Lilly, is a real copy of him…" Matt drew in a deep breath and continued his case.

"As soon as we saw her, we thought she could be his granddaughter, cos he came on holiday to Spain many times with us, you know? And he ran off a couple of times. Maybe met up with a girlfriend and you know dogs… So… she could be related!"

Lucy looked up at her brother and I guess she realised for the first time that he too, really wanted Lilly. He was just shy about his feelings.

The woman finally waved the boys away. They couldn't wait to get back to the square. Then she looked me straight in the eye.

"The truth is…", she said, "we can't look after the dog. You see the balcony at the top of this building?"

We all looked up. It was really high. Three or four stories, I reckoned. She continued.

"That's our flat. I have four children. My husband works all hours and I run a business from home. I can't deal with a dog. It's that simple. She is no trouble and adorable as you know, but it's not fair on her."

# CHAPTER 29

# I DON’T BELIEVE IT!

Despite all of her confession, I don’t think any of us were ready for her next statement. I gave Lucy’s hand another squeeze. She looked at me with her eyes full of water. I knew she was trying so hard to be brave.

That was when the woman said –

“If you want her, you can have her.”

Just like that.

“I will need to speak to my husband over the weekend, ‘cos he is mighty fond of her, but he’s at work all day, and doesn’t have to deal with everything. You understand, don’t you?"

Lucy broke her hands free from Nan and myself and threw herself into her mum’s body, wrapping her arms around her waist.

“She's mine, mum, she’s mine!”, she cried. “I knew it, I knew it!” She promptly released herself from Kathy and picked the sweet dog up off the ground and whirled around and around with her in the air.

“Right!”, said Nan to the woman, “we’ll be back on Monday morning first thing.”

We all took it in turn to give our little friend a big cuddle. Lucy whispered something into her ears but that was between her and the dog. I thought I heard her saying something about three sunrises.

"So, it's Millylilly. That has to be her name," cried Lucy, "It's a lovely name!" And she repeated it all the way home!

It was great news. Matt, too, began repeating the dog's new name.

"Fingers crossed for Monday, then!" said Kathy.

"B'jesus," remarked Nan, "I didn't see that coming, fancy giving her away, eh? I mean, aren't we the lucky ones?"

She was so right! And if she could have skipped with her two new plastic knees, she and Lucy would have been skipping all the way home.

Monday morning could not come quick enough. I wasn't one hundred percent sure of the outcome, and I know Nan and Kathy were thinking the same, but Lucy was convinced, as she always had been, that Millylilly was destined to be with her forever.

We drove down and Kathy and Matt directed us around the narrow streets, until we were finally at the door.

Over the weekend, we discussed how we were going to transport Millylilly back to England.

Kathy and the children were flying home in a few days and we were going rambling through Europe in our camper van en route to England a week later.

"Let's wait and see what happens on Monday," said Nan, as cautious as ever.

# CHAPTER 30

# BURIED KNUCKLES AND BONES

I had never before returned home to Ireland without Bendog being there to greet me.

Nan picked me up as usual, this time without Bendog in the back trying desperately to clamber through to greet me with a big wet lick.

I realized how hard it must have been for Nan, being at the cottage all this time, hoping that he'd turn up, listening for any noise or a familiar rattle as when he plunged himself through the dog flap, covered in bog water and filth and - to our horror-shook himself in the middle of the kitchen.

Or his incessant loud barking when he had sprung frogs in the bog wet soggy land in the garden at the back of the house.

Nan filled me in with all her news as normal but all I wanted to hear was news of my missing boy. She must have sensed my preoccupation.

"I think we have to accept he's gone, I'm afraid Jack".

I could feel my shoulders curl forward and my head droop forward.

We didn't talk again until we turned into the road where we had lost him.

I burst into tears, and Nan stopped the car. It was unbearable revisiting this site again but it was our only way up to the cottage. The memories of the feelings engulfing me that fateful night - and since - came flooding back.

My heart was sinking, remembering how we searched all night, calling his name… But to no avail… And having to return home without him… Oh! It was all too hard.

It would be two years later when I finally had the courage to accept Bendog was never going to return to me. And so, I set about to dig a plot in his favourite bog-garden.

I started collecting up all his belongings as I found them. They were so special… His toys, old worn leads, collars, and plenty of old chewed knuckles. Also bones he'd hidden under the sacks and wood piles in the shed.

And on Mothers' day 2013, I erected a recycled metal cross, put all his belongings into the hole and filled it in.

And I will, I'm sure at some point soon, when the children are home, collectively arrange his photo and write a special message in his memory and attach it to the pole saying a prayer of thanksgiving. No doubt.

And I will rejoice in a celebration of his life with our one and only beloved Bendog.

I often look out on the television especially when a programme is on relating to those countries 'down under' to see if I spot a black and white Springer Spaniel coming up from the ground having eventually dug a hole deep enough to facilitate his arrival in someone's back garden.

At least I'd know what he'd been up to these past few years.

# CHAPTER 31

# THE RISING SUN

Monday morning couldn't come quick enough for Lucy. If she asked us once she asked us a dozen times how much longer until Monday morning.

“How many suns have you seen appear over the pool since Friday, Lucy?" asked clever Matt. He loved anything to do with science or astronomy, as long as we stuck to the facts.

“Well", said Lucy looking up to the sky, her finger resting on her chin. "Mum sent me up to the solarium to bring some of her washing down so she could pack her case for England on Tuesday. Now let’s see… that was… hummm… Saturday and I saw it rise over the famous Pink Lakes and - she continued - today is Sunday and we went to the market early and I saw it from the van window peeping over the mountain, so it’s tomorrow we have to go!” Lucy eyes were almost popping from her face.

“YES! Millylilly’s coming home! Millylilly’s coming home!”, she sang at the top of her voice and it sounded so sweet and tuneful.

Matt interrupted her.

“Yes, that's right Lucy, as long as we don’t have a total eclipse tonight.” He sounded triumphant and worldly.

Lucy stopped in mid track, her eyes narrowed, her lips taught and unhumoured.

"What's one of those?" she inquired, looking suddenly daunted. It wasn't the first time her brother had spouted out an unexplainable fact, though.

"It's nothing Lucy, nothing to worry about." I said.

"Whatever the outcome, we will be on the doorstep by first light. Ok?" I was hoping to reassure her. At the same time I just knew she had her hopes set very high, convinced as she has always been, that Millylilly was destined to be with her forever.

Lucy, smiling at Matt, continued more of her new rendition of the homecoming of Millylilly, making it up as she went along.

Nan and Kathy, who had been putting away the market purchases during this uncomfortable moment, called me over to the terrace.

"What do you think? Will he, won't he?", whispered Kathy, her eyebrows meeting in the middle, a frown I was not familiar with. Yes, those were the questions milling around in my head too.

And I know it was the same for Nan, as we discussed the practicalities of getting Millylilly back to the UK, should it all turn out well.

# CHAPTER 32

# MILLYLILLY'S PLAN

*I can't believe I'm back here again. So much for living the dream! Nothing has changed. Everything is as I left it…*

I put my head down and grabbed the string of my new sombrero under my chin with my paw. I was able to pull it over my mouth so I could take it off when I wanted to.

*Well, this is much better than my old one,* I thought. It was a much better fit but I knew that it must go back on top if I got one squeak from those kids.

I've left on my frilly waistband. It's silly I know, but it helps me feel closer to Lucy.

*Right!*

I had a plan, a strategy to get me through the next few days. Eat, sleep and dream of Lucy! If the Mr. came to visit, I'm going to be giving him the cold shoulder too. *That's it! AND if I get disturbed by any one of those brats I will growl and growl until they leave me alone. Roll on Monday!*

I lifted my head up and stared at the building across the road.

I will just be able to see the sunrise three times.

Just like Lucy said.

# CHAPTER 33

# ADIOS AMIGOS!

Monday morning bright and early, everyone in the house was up and ready to go. We drove down to the village and Kathy and Matt directed us around the narrow streets until we were finally at the front door.

I took great pleasure in revving the engine just to let them know we had arrived. We hadn't even turned off the engine when the woman appeared from the flat. She stood on the pavement, her lips tight together, stoney faced, fidgeting with her dress.

"Oh no, this is not good news", I confided in Nan who was preparing her legs for disembarkation. She glanced at me and raised her eyes.

"Everyone out!!" she roared.

As the sliding door slowly opened and Lucy was about to jump, Millylilly galloped through the legs of the woman and flung her little body at Lucy, nearly knocking her back into the van.

The woman turned into the doorway and followed Millylilly, carrying a dog's bed, a few chewed toys and a bag of dried food.

"Oh, thank goodness for that!" I exclaimed to Nan, our collective apparent relief from all the smiling at one another with the sight of the woman helping Matt put the dog's property into the back of the van.

“Thank you”, we all said in unison.

“No. Thank YOU!” said the woman.” Adios Milly!” she called as we all waved goodbye.

I put my foot down hard onto the accelerator and drove off hastily just in case she changed her mind.

“You see everyone, I CAN talk dog”, exclaimed Lucy as she held Millylilly close to her chest.

“Ok Lucy”, said Matt, “maybe you can! Maybe!”

“Just one small query” said Kathy. "How are you going to get her back to the UK?"

“No problem”, said Nan, “we’ll take her back with us, won't we children? But we’re going all the way through five European countries first!”

“It’s going to take a lot of preparation, this voyage of ours” replied Matt.

I could imagine his mind already compiling a list of on-board essentials.

“It’ll be one PAWSOME adventure!”, cried Lucy, placing a huge kiss on the dog’s forehead.

*Yes, indeed* , I thought.

But then again, that’s another story!

# EPILOGUE

This story is grounded in many true facts throughout the book. Although places and characters' names have been changed, the fundamental truth provided by the story leaves the family pondering four plausible explanations. There is a possibility that Millylilly is, in fact a descendant of Bendog.

After all he had holidayed many times at the villa during his life and had gone *walkabout* on his own at times, not straying too far, but enough time to procreate!

Could it be divine intervention, aware of our suffering and playing the part of comforter after our sad loss of Bendog? Or a feeling of possible re-incarnation across 2500 miles? Or simply a coincidence that this young dog escaped at the same time we were on holiday, finding us as she did? That was in itself quite a phenomena!

Whatever the reason, the loss of my old boy Bendog and the rescuing of the beautiful young Millylilly has been well worth the emotional rollercoaster ride.

And although no other dog could replace our old boy, meeting Millylilly has only served to open our hearts even wider.

# THE AUTHOR

Pauline Edmunds is a semi-retired nurse. She shares her nomadic lifestyle with her godchildren and travels in a campervan between her cottage in Co Donegal, Ireland and THE REST OF THE WORLD.

www.ingramcontent.com/pod-product-compliance
Lightning Source LLC
Chambersburg PA
CBHW060948050426
42337CB00052B/1876
*9780993167102*